D0427017

MY GOD,

DO YOU

LOVE

ME?

MY GOD,

A Woman's

DO YOU

Conversations

LOVE

With God

ME?

BRENDA HUNTER, PH.D.

WATERBROOK
PRESS

COLORADO SPRINGS

MY GOD, DO YOU LOVE ME?
PUBLISHED BY WATERBROOK PRESS
5446 North Academy Boulevard, Suite 200
Colorado Springs, Colorado 80918
A division of Bantam Doubleday Dell Publishing Group, Inc.

Scriptures in this book, unless otherwise noted, are from the *Holy Bible,
New International Version* copyright ©1973, 1978, 1984, International
Bible Society, Zondervan Bible Publishers. Used by permission; all rights
reserved. The scriptures that appear in italics represent the author's emphasis.

ISBN 1-57856-030-6

Copyright © 1998 by Brenda Hunter, Ph.D.

All rights reserved. No part of this book may be reproduced or transmitted
in any form or by any means, electronic or mechanical, including photocopying,
recording, or by any information storage and retrieval system, without permission
in writing from the publisher.

Printed in the United States of America.
1998—First Edition

10 9 8 7 6 5 4 3 2 1

Lord, to whom could I dedicate this book but you?
Thank you that you have heard the cries of my heart
and have shown me in countless ways that you love me.

CONTENTS

Contents

A Woman's Conversations with God

How does any writer choose her subject? I suspect that most of us who write for a living write about what's closest to home: our current struggles, our emotional pain, often our past. Most of the books I have written have evolved from my life, both inner and outer. Like the one you hold in your hands, those books were written in an attempt to make sense out of my personal life and spiritual journey—a journey that has been, by turns, exhilarating, maddening, confusing, joyful.

I started writing *My God, Do You Love Me?* years ago at a time when I felt particularly vulnerable. I was skidding into my forties and a period I later came to call "the hormonal crazies"; as my estrogen levels rose and fell, my marital problems also seemed to crest and abate. My two wonderful daughters, who had been my boon companions during their early childhood, suddenly became obstreperous teenagers—daily, hourly, asserting their independence. Some days they were quite rejecting. In the middle of all this, our family moved from New Jersey to Washington, D.C., and I found myself suddenly friendless and lonely. God alone became my daily companion, my most reliable and comforting friend, as Don headed for the office and the girls left each morning for school.

As I read my Bible in the quiet of those mornings, I decided to write down my feelings and look for God's answers in Scripture. I needed to know that he understood my emotional pain and that he cared deeply about all that concerned me. Thus began daily written conversations with God that helped me cope with my life's stresses. In time I put my notebook aside though I continued to meet with God most mornings.

In the intervening years, I received a doctorate in psychology, worked on my marriage, and helped launch my daughters into adulthood. I also began a career as a therapist, working with women who struggled with depression, anxiety, childhood pain, difficulties in their intimate relationships, and low self-esteem. As I listened to my clients, I realized that I had been where many of them were, struggling with a core life question: "My God, do you love me?" They, like me, went on to ask, "If you love me, why do you afflict me?" and "If you hear me, why are you so often silent?"

I worked to help my clients understand that God did indeed love them and that he alone could heal their deepest wounds and help them rework their painful pasts. As their therapist, I empathized with their hurts, validated their feelings, and tried to help them achieve greater wholeness.

I felt confident of God's love for my patients and myself and fairly secure in my faith until last April— Good Friday, to be exact—when I rolled over in bed and discovered a lump in my right breast. Suddenly my world upended. Facing surgery and an array of invasive treatment options, I was terrified, confused, and overwhelmed. Once again I felt exquisitely vulnerable and alone. Only this time the stakes were higher than ever before. My life was, and is, on the line. Breast cancer is a fearsome foe, and only the Lord truly understands my middle-of-the-night terror and my desperate need to know that he daily holds me in the palm of his hand. Although my family has been wonderfully empathic and supportive, only God can get inside my mind and understand the intense emotions that ricochet from happiness to fear, sometimes within the space of an hour.

Intuitively, I understood that I would begin to find inner peace if I again wrote down my conversations with God. So I took my old notebook and went to Glory Ridge, just outside Asheville, North Carolina, two months after a mastectomy. God provided that place of retreat—a log cabin on sixty-two acres of forest where I could hike, sit in the sun, pick succulent blackberries, and listen to the sounds of nature. Each night as I lay on my bed, I listened to cicadas thunder like phalanxes of advancing soldiers. Only as the sun rose over the mountains did they lapse into silence. One night coon dogs chased nocturnal raccoons on the ridge, barking all night while Heidi, the huge St. Bernard that guarded the place, ranged over the property, protecting her own but also jarring me from sleep hour by hour. The next morning I felt as if my head had been hit by a hammer—so much for this suburban woman's erroneous belief in the tranquillity of nature!

I went alone to pour out my pain and to begin listening to God, as I had done seventeen years before. I needed to hear his voice, to speak from my heart to him and know that he heard me. Each morning I sat at a tiny, weathered table on a small, screened-in porch just off the kitchen, surrounded by deep woods and noisy birds and insects. I am not a sensing person, but I found it a healing experience to be so tuned in to nature. As I spoke to God and listened intently for his answers, I discovered anew that he is never far from our side—that he hears our desperate daytime prayers and our middle-of-the-night whispers.

So it is from this place of personal suffering that I have put pen to paper and come before the Lord. It has been my hope that as I have asked him questions from my own human heart, as well as questions I have heard my clients ask him, I would speak for you. Each life has its own particular crises and struggles, and some are more severe than others. But we all struggle with our intimate relationships, our disappointments, our self-images, and our longing to be known and loved just as we are. All of us, whether married or single, have those moments when we are afraid. That's when we need to know that God cares deeply for us in an intimate and personal way. So whether you're a young woman or a grandmother like I am, I believe this little book has something to say to you about your uniqueness to God.

Within these pages, I have tried to capture the intimacy of a woman's honest relationship with her God. When she speaks about what's in her heart—jealousy, anxiety, fear, joy—he always answers. The scriptural selections are sometimes paraphrased but most often cited directly. Direct quotations (drawn from the New International Version of the Bible) are always italicized.

Long ago when I published my first book, *Beyond Divorce,* Dick Baltzell negotiated my contract and challenged me to write openly. Honestly. "No tears in the writer, no tears in the reader," he said. Well, dear reader, I have written this book with deep emotion and occasional tears but also with a growing realization that God will carry me through my current struggles just as he has done in the past. I am not alone in my fiery trials; nor, my friend, are you.

BRENDA HUNTER, PH.D.

VIENNA, VA

1

MY GOD, DO YOU LOVE ME— TRULY LOVE ME?

When I doubt that you hear my cries,
when I feel I am one of billions of humans
inhabiting this planet,
it's hard to feel special to you.
Do you frown at such times,
or do you hear my longing to know
I have a loving, responsive Father?

Are you aware of my struggle
to feel I have worth in your eyes,
especially when I knowingly sin
or fail to live up to my own expectations?

Ah, Father—

Are you privy to the childhood pain,
to the memories I haven't been able to exorcise?
Do you witness my attempts to connect emotionally
with my husband, children, close friends—
attempts that sometimes falter?

What do you think of my drivenness—
my breathless attempts to impress others
with my accomplishments and good deeds?

And do you judge me as harshly as I judge myself,
or do you carry me and my concerns
in some small corner of your vast heart,
tenderly watching over me
as a mother watches over her child?

I need to know where we stand, Lord.
I need to feel I am not alone.
I need to know that you care,
that you love me
with an intense, enduring love
that will carry me softly into eternity.

My God, do you love *even* me?

"I have loved you with an everlasting love;
I have drawn you with loving-kindness.
As a mother comforts her child,
so will I comfort you.
Since you are precious and honored in my sight,
and because I love you,
I will give men in exchange for you,
and people in exchange for your life.
Do not be afraid, for I am with you.
Though the mountains be shaken

and the hills be removed,
yet my unfailing love for you will not be shaken
nor my covenant of peace be removed,"
says the LORD, who has compassion on you.

JEREMIAH 31:3, ISAIAH 66:13, 43:4-5, 54:10

Know therefore that the LORD your God is God;
he is the faithful God, keeping his covenant of
love to a thousand generations of those
who love him and keep his commands.

DEUTERONOMY 7:9

2

TODAY I FEEL DISCOURAGED AND DEPRESSED

Lord,
Things are just not going according to plan.
My *life* hasn't gone according to plan!
When I look back over the past week (or year or
    decade),
I see that many of my expectations,
plans, and ambitions have been foiled.
Broken dreams lie in shards at my feet.

I feel like those ancient believers
on the road to Emmaus.
They, too, were desperately discouraged.
Jesus,
the carrier of dreams,
had not been crowned king.
He dared to die and, in dying,
thwarted their human agendas and
destroyed their plans.

"But we had hoped—" they cried.
"But I had hoped—" I cry.

They had hoped that Christ
would redeem Israel—but on their terms.
Overwhelmed by disappointment,
they failed to recognize their Lord,
though he walked beside them
in resurrected form on that dusty road to Emmaus.

Ah, Father—

How often have I, too, failed
to recognize the living Christ
walking the road beside me!
How often have I said, "But I had hoped—"

Open my eyes to recognize Jesus
just as you opened the eyes of the believers
on the road to Emmaus.
And may I, like they, have
a heart that burns within me
simply because I have walked with Christ.
Let me exclaim—as they did—
"It is true! The Lord has risen"—
in history and in my heart.

As I come to you with a listening heart, Lord,
what will you say to me?

"For I know the plans I have for you,"
declares the LORD, "plans to prosper you
and not to harm you, plans to give you
hope and a future."

BRENDA HUNTER

"For my thoughts are not your thoughts,
neither are your ways my ways," declares the LORD.
"As the heavens are higher than the earth,
so are my ways higher than your ways
and my thoughts than your thoughts."

LUKE 24:13-35, JEREMIAH 29:11, ISAIAH 55:8-9

"Have I not commanded you? Be strong and courageous.
Do not be terrified; do not be discouraged, for the LORD
your God will be with you wherever you go."

JOSHUA 1:9

6

3

WHERE DO I GO TO FIND MEANING AND PURPOSE?

Lord,
I need a sense of meaning and purpose.
Today the ordinariness of my life
seeps into my very soul.
I feel I have lost touch
with my deepest self, my dreams,
        the intrinsic purpose of my life.
Instead I fritter away the hours
doing, running, talking, fretting.
Is this why you created me—
    just to work this job,
    run my household,
    take care of my family?

Father, I lose myself daily
in phone calls, conversations with friends,
the myriad tasks before me.
But in the dark of night—
long after my husband and children sleep—
I come to you with open, empty hands, asking,
        "Is this all there is to my life?"

I long to know that you created
me for a singular purpose—
that you designed me
to give something to others
that's unique, that bears your imprint,
while coming through the prism of my personality.
For I shall meet you face to face someday.
And when that happens,
I long to stand before your throne, unashamed.
I want to bask in the warmth of your smile.

Please speak to me, Lord, about why you
        created me in the first place.

Thank you that your word tells me that
you chose me before the creation
of the world to be holy and blameless in your sight—
In love you predestined me
to be adopted as your child through Jesus Christ,
in accordance with your pleasure and will.
In Christ I was also chosen, having been predestined
in conformity with the purpose of your will.

For I am your workmanship,
created in Christ Jesus to do good works,
works which you prepared in advance
for me to do.

O Father, thank you
that it's not all up to me—

that I don't have to imbue every moment
of my life with color, meaning, and purpose
but that I can simply come to you
with empty hands and an open heart—
and trust that it is you who works in me
both to will and to act according to your
  good purpose.

I fling my life up to you, O Lord,
and ask you
to fill it with your special meaning and your
  purposes.
Your love. Your joy.
I will wait on you.

EPHESIANS 1:4-5, 2:10, PHILIPPIANS 2:13

Now to him who is able to do immeasurably
more than all we ask or imagine,
according to his power that is at work
within us, to him be glory in the church and
in Christ Jesus throughout all generations,
for ever and ever! Amen.

EPHESIANS 3:20-21

4

SOMETIMES I'M SO AFRAID, LORD

Some days I'm so afraid, though I may not show it.
Illness strikes.
Money is tight.
A child is battling an intense, inner struggle.
I find, after I have talked to all my comforters,
I still must hear from you.
They are only human.
You alone see the whole picture.

But how *do* you see this situation, Lord?
What do you want me to think about
this particular trial that strikes fear
in my deepest heart?
When fear has me by the throat,
when I feel lost in the backside of the desert,
can I count on you?
Will you see me through
this fiery trial that threatens to undo me?

Are you *here,* Lord?
Are you *with* me, Lord?

"Fear not, for I have redeemed you;
I have summoned you by name; you are mine.
When you pass through the waters,
I will be with you;
and when you pass through the rivers,
they will not sweep over you.
When you walk through the fire,
you will not be burned;
the flames will not set you ablaze.
For I am the LORD, your God,
the Holy One of Israel, your Savior.
Do not be afraid, for I am with you.

"I will pour out my Spirit on your offspring,
and my blessing on your descendants.
Is there any God besides me?
No, there is no other Rock; I know not one."

Thank you, Lord, for the immeasurable
comfort of your presence.

I can face anything today with my hand in yours.

ISAIAH 43:1-3,5; 44:3,8

"Do not be afraid, but let your hands be strong."

ZECHARIAH 8:13

When I am afraid, I will trust in you.
In God, whose word I praise, in God I trust;
I will not be afraid. What can mortal man
do to me?

PSALM 56:3-4

5

TODAY MY HEART IS GRATEFUL, LORD

As I feel the sun on my back,
      hear the buzzing of flies
      outside this tiny, screened-in porch,
      and gaze on patches of sunshine
      bathing nearby trees,
I am grateful for the constancy
of your love and care.
You have brought me through the night
and given me another day to worship you.
Truly, this is your day.
You have created it, and we can enjoy
it together.

The wonder of life and breath!
The beauty of sunshine!
The glory of your love for me!
Like King David, I dance
before you in the moment.
It's all that I have for sure.

For Jesus said, *"Do not worry about tomorrow,*
for tomorrow will worry about itself.
Each day has enough trouble of its own."

So I choose to throw my whole heart into living
    this day to the full.
Thank you that though
there are difficulties in my life
I can still rejoice
in this singular moment,
knowing it will never come again.
Thank you, Father, that I am alive!

Lord,
may I sing with the psalmist—
It is good to praise the LORD
and make music to your name,
O Most High,
to proclaim your love
in the morning and your faithfulness at night,
to the music of the ten-stringed lyre
and the melody of the harp.

Lord, your compassions never fail.
They are new every morning;
great is your faithfulness.

Today I want to bask
in your great, unfailing love,

trusting you with an uncertain future,
believing
that you will be with me in all my tomorrows,
just as you are with me today.

MATTHEW 6:34; PSALM 92:1-3; LAMENTATIONS 3:22-23,32

The LORD is my strength and my shield; my heart trusts in him, and I am helped. My heart leaps for joy and I will give thanks to him in song.

PSALM 28:7

6

HELP ME LOVE MY HUSBAND

Lord, help me to love this man—
this husband I have chosen as my life's companion.
Some days we live and work
together in synchrony,
and feelings of love wash over me.
At such times I am grateful to you and to him
for the husband and father he has become.
Other days—when he hurts me or we strongly
    disagree—
I find him stubborn, defensive,
unable to hear what I am trying
so desperately to share from my deepest self.
The words beneath the words.
He tells me he struggles just as hard
to communicate with
stubborn, defensive me.
He urges me to express my needs
in softer tones, ever mindful of his feelings.
"Men are tender plants," he sighs.
"Besides," he says, "I'm not a therapist.
I'm just a man."

Some days I just want to be carried
close to this man's heart.
His best friend.
His confidante.
But at other times, Lord,
I want to flee to a convent
or sail to a deserted island.
Sometimes I just need time alone to think my own
    thoughts.
Sometimes I need my women friends.

What am I to do with this man
who lives trustingly beside me?
How can we live together
in greater harmony
and joy?

Ah, Lord, you tell me to
be completely humble and gentle.
Your Word reminds me
that I must be patient, bearing with this man in love,
making *every effort*
to keep the unity of the Spirit through
the bond of peace.

Help me, Lord. Clothe me with *compassion,*
kindness, humility, gentleness and patience—
all those virtues I lack.
Help us to *bear with each other and forgive*

whatever grievances we have against one another.
Only with your help, Father, can I
forgive him as completely as you have forgiven me.
Only in the power of your Holy Spirit
can I pursue love and unity
rather than self-interest.

Ah, Lord, your Word tells me
that I must submit to my husband as unto you—
for the husband is the head of the wife
as Christ is the head of the church, his body,
of which he is the Savior.
Now as the church submits to Christ,
so also wives should submit to their husbands
in everything.

Everything, Lord?
That's hard for this woman to do.

Yet you have called my husband
to a task greater than mine.
He is to love me
as Christ loved the church
and gave himself up for her to make her holy,
cleansing her by the washing with water
through the word, and to present her to
himself as a radiant church,
without stain or wrinkle or any other blemish,
but holy and blameless.

That's a lot for him to do.

Beginning today, Lord,
help me to reverence and respect this man
who is called to love me as he loves himself.
We are one flesh.
Please make us one heart.

EPHESIANS 4:2-3; COLOSSIANS 3:12-14; EPHESIANS 5:22-27,33

Your beauty should not come from
outward adornment, such as braided hair
and the wearing of gold jewelry and fine clothes.
Instead, it should be that of your inner self,
the unfading beauty of a gentle and quiet spirit,
which is of great worth in God's sight.

For this is the way the holy women of the past
who put their hope in God used
to make themselves beautiful.

They were submissive to their own husbands,
like Sarah, who obeyed Abraham
and called him her master.

You are her daughters if you do what is right
and do not give way to fear.

1 PETER 3:3-6

7

GIVE ME
AN UNDIVIDED HEART, LORD

I long to be your fruitful child,
      to love you with all of my heart,
        mind, soul, and strength.
But I am so easily distracted.
I lack discipline…
some days I fritter away the time
I have set aside for you.
A friend calls, and I am wooed
into the warmth of female companionship;
the hour I have set aside for you slips away.
The baby has a fitful night,
so I stay in bed an hour longer,
praying she and I will sleep.

There have been those days, months—years—
when I have quietly gone my own way.
I may have looked like your child
as I attended church and helped others.
But inwardly I worshiped
at the idols of my own
di-
vid-

ed heart—
Longing for praise and recognition.
Yearning for the big house, exotic vacations.
Needing accomplished children to
make me feel like a good mother.
Lusting for kudos from those I respect.

But I'm learning, Lord.
Sometimes I struggle under the rod
of your discipline.
But you
are a father who
disciplines us for our own good
so that we may share in your holiness.
You assure me that
no discipline seems pleasant
at the time, but painful.
Later on, however, it produces a
harvest of righteousness and peace for those
who have been trained by it.

Set me free from the things that bind me—
the idols of my heart.
Teach me your way, O LORD,
and I will walk in your truth;
give me an undivided heart,
that I may fear your name.

Capture me, Lord,
and I shall be finally free.

"Forget the former things;
do not dwell on the past.
See, I am doing a new thing!
Now it springs up; do you not perceive it?
I, even I, am he who
blots out your transgressions,
for my own sake, and
remembers your sins no more.
I am the LORD, and there is no other;
apart from me there is no God.
I will strengthen you,
though you have not acknowledged me,
so that from the rising of the sun
to the place of its setting
men may know there is none besides me.
I am the LORD, and there is no other.
I, the LORD, do all these things.
You will seek me and find me
when you seek me with all your heart."

HEBREWS 12:10-11; PSALM 86:11;
ISAIAH 43:18-19,25; 45:5-7; JEREMIAH 29:13

"I will give them an undivided heart
and put a new spirit in them;
I will remove from them their heart of stone
and give them a heart of flesh."

EZEKIEL 11:19

8

SOMETIMES I FEEL LIKE
A MOTHERLESS CHILD

Today I feel
vulnerable.
Dependent.
Depressed.
But when I feel this way, Lord,
I don the mask of the independent,
together, invincible woman,
fooling friends and even my husband.
I hide my neediness
too well away,
        sometimes even from myself.

At these times, I withdraw
        from close friends—
They haven't walked in my shoes.
How could they possibly understand?
Besides, they seem lost in family,
        children's activities, sports, or career.
Busy, busy, busy—
too busy, I feel, for me.

During these painful moments,
I feel like Isaiah's bruised reed
      about to break,
or a smoldering wick
      about to be snuffed out.

So, Lord, I come to you.
El Shaddai,
the tender, nurturing God.
I'm needy just now.
What will you say to me today, Lord?

"Can a mother forget the baby at her breast
and have no compassion
on the child she has borne?
Though she may forget,
I will not forget you!
See, I have engraved you
on the palms of my hands;
your walls are ever before me.

"I said, 'You are my servant'; I have chosen you
and have not rejected you.
So do not fear, for I am with you;
do not be dismayed, for I am your God.
I will strengthen you and help you;
I will uphold you with my righteous right hand.

"Never will I leave you;
never will I forsake you."

Thank you, Lord, for your life-giving, encouraging
  words.
Today, and always, I will carry them close to my
  heart.

ISAIAH 42:3, 49:15-16, 41:9-10, HEBREWS 13:5

For this is what the LORD says:
"I will extend peace to her like a river,
and the wealth of nations like a flooding stream;
you will nurse and be carried on her arm
and dandled on her knees.
As a mother comforts her child,
so will I comfort you."

ISAIAH 66:12-13

9

YOU CARRY ME ACROSS THE YEARS

Thank you, O my Lord,
that I can flee to the shelter of your wings
to rest in your shadow this day.

You have always been with me.
Unseen but felt.
I remember, long before I ever heard about Jesus
or understood that I needed a Savior,
lying in the lush grass as a child
during the halcyon days of summer,
gazing up at the clouds floating overhead,
aware that you were watching over me.

During the good times and the bad,
I have sensed your presence in my life.
Whenever I have come to you—
repentant, hurt, needy, or happy—
you have been there for me.
Sometimes I have come to complain
about rebellious children,
marital troubles,
financial woes,

loneliness.
Always you have listened.
And I know you are listening today.
Once again, Lord, I have come to a river
I cannot cross alone.
I need you to send me an angel—
or a boat—or both—
to get to the other side.

I have lived long enough to know
that you will hear and answer.
I know…
> You never give me what I deserve.
> You protect a mother's children
> when she prays a heartfelt prayer.
> You heal marriages trapped in
> a cul-de-sac, and
> you develop submitted talents.

We have come a long way, Lord, you and I.
We have quite a history.

As I face this new crisis,
increase my faith to believe that
just as you have been with me in the past,
so you will be with me in the present moment of
confusion and darkness.
Will you carry me today and in the days ahead
as a father carries his child so I will not feel
so frightened and alone?

"I am the LORD your God,
who brought you out of Egypt.
You shall acknowledge no God but me,
no Savior except me.
I cared for you in the desert,
in the land of burning heat.

"Listen to me, O house of Jacob,
all you who remain of the house of Israel,
you whom I have upheld
since you were conceived,
and have carried since your birth.

"Even to your old age and gray hairs
I am he,
I am he who will sustain you.
I have made you and I will carry you;
I will sustain you and I will rescue you.

"I will betroth you to me forever."

HOSEA 13:4-5, ISAIAH 46:3-4, HOSEA 2:19

Cast your cares on the LORD and he will sustain you;
he will never let the righteous fall.

PSALM 55:22

10

HELP ME, LORD,
WITH SLEEPLESS NIGHTS

O Father,
I had another sleepless night.
Exhausted from the day, eager for rest,
I lay in bed, ruminating for hours.

Worries flooded my mind;
my body couldn't relax.
It's hard to lie awake when the world is quiet
and my husband sleeps peacefully beside me.
Like the psalmist, in my wakefulness,
I have become like a bird alone on a roof.
At such times I cry out to you,
reminding you that the psalmist says you
grant sleep to those you love.

But if you want me awake,
then help me to meditate on you during the
dark and lonely nighttime hours.
At Gethsemane
Christ prayed well into the night,
and, according to legend, Saint Francis often

awoke in the middle of the night
to go into the forest to pray.

Lord, help me to understand that
even when I can't sleep,
I can still *rest in the shadow of the Almighty.*
Instead of being distressed,
help me to say with the psalmist,
In the night I remember your name, O LORD,
that I may meditate on your promises.

PSALM 102:7; 127:2; 91:1; 119:55,148

"Come to me, all you who are weary and burdened,
and I will give you rest."

MATTHEW 11:28

11

FATHER, IF YOU LOVE ME, WHY DO YOU AFFLICT ME?

This year my trials just keep coming—
Relentlessly, inexorably, like phalanxes of soldiers
advancing against a walled city.
Hammering against gates that groan and threaten
    to collapse.
Repeatedly, I come running to you, Lord, asking,
        How am I to understand suffering—
           my own and the pain of others?

Just yesterday I heard of a baby
struggling with kidney cancer
and of a teacher, married
with two small children, who
is dying of a brain tumor.
Even now I watch a friend,
a forty-two-year-old mother of three,
fight for her life against invasive cancer
that has metastasized to her brain, liver, and bones.

Lord, where are you?
Why don't you protect your children from harm's way?
How are we to understand calamities?

How am I to face my own
severe struggle?

I run to your Word.
I read:
Do not be surprised
at the painful trial you are suffering,
as though something strange
were happening to you.
But rejoice that you
participate in the sufferings of Christ,
so that you may be overjoyed
when his glory is revealed.
Those who suffer according to God's will
should commit themselves to their faithful Creator
and continue to do good.

Consider it pure joy…whenever you face trials of many
    kinds,
because…the testing of your faith
develops perseverance.

And once perseverance has completed its work,
your Word promises I will be mature, complete,
    lacking nothing.

How I long to be strong and mature in you.
But just now I desperately need your help
to understand the enormity of human suffering.

Thank you that you are not an unfeeling God!
Thank you for caring when your children are
    afflicted and grieve.
Thank you that when his good friend
Lazarus died, *Jesus wept.*
Although he knew
he could raise Lazarus from the dead,
Christ was still deeply troubled because he loved
    his friend
and knew death was an enemy.

Father, keep me praying, trusting, and
looking to you for help in my current situation.
May I rest the full weight of my suffering
on you since you care for me deeply.
And may I continue to pray for my friend.

Whatever happens to her or to me,
I am grateful that Christ said:
"I am the resurrection and the life.
He who believes in me will live,
even though he dies;
and whoever lives and believes in me
will never die."

1 PETER 4:12-13,19; JAMES 1:2-4; JOHN 11:33,35,25-26

33

*Although the Lord gives you the bread of adversity and the
water of affliction, your teachers will be hidden no more;
with your own eyes you will see them.*

*The moon will shine like the sun, and the sunlight
will be seven times brighter, like the light of seven
full days, when the LORD binds up the bruises of
his people and heals the wounds he inflicted.*

ISAIAH 30:20,26

*For men are not cast off by the Lord forever.
Though he brings grief, he will show compassion,
so great is his unfailing love.
For he does not willingly bring affliction or grief
to the children of men.*

LAMENTATIONS 3:31-33

12

LET ME BE YOUR SERVANT, LORD

Yesterday I asked my hostess,
 a vibrant sixty-nine-year-old
 who owns the cabin where I'm staying,
if I could use her washing machine (my cabin has
 none).

 "Let me be your servant today," she said.

I protested.
She insisted.

I agreed,
 embarrassed that she should wash and fold
 my scruffy underwear, Bermuda shorts,
 and towels while I wrote.
Hours later, when she felt she
would not break my concentration,
she reappeared, laundry basket in hand,
my clothes folded *and* pressed.

 "Thank you," she said,
 "for allowing me to be your servant today."

Her words stopped me dead in my tracks.

Lord,
how long has it been since
I even thought about being anybody's servant?
Granted, I care for my husband,
children, aging mother, and others.
Sometimes with great reluctance.
But become their servant?

Thank you for this woman's object lesson,
for reminding me that Christ,
who possessed your nature,
took on himself the humble garb of humanity.
Your Word says that I should
imitate the humility of Christ,
who, being in very nature God,
did not consider equality with God
something to be grasped,
but made himself nothing,
taking the very nature of a servant,
being made in human likeness.
And being found in appearance as a man,
he humbled himself
and became obedient to death—
even death on a cross!
Therefore God exalted him to the highest place
and gave him the name
that is above every name,
that at the name of Jesus

every knee should bow,
in heaven and on earth
and under the earth,
and every tongue confess that
Jesus Christ is Lord,
to the glory of God the father.

If Christ came to earth and became a servant,
what does this say about my desire to be served?
If he humbled himself completely,
shouldn't I?

May I never forget that Jesus said,
"Whoever wants to become great among you
must be your servant,
and whoever wants to be first must be slave of all."

Help me, Lord, to become your servant this day.
Joyfully. Unreservedly. Wholeheartedly.

PHILIPPIANS 2:6-11, MARK 10:43-44

Serve wholeheartedly, as if you were serving the Lord,
not men, because you know that the Lord will reward
everyone for whatever good he does, whether he is
slave or free.

EPHESIANS 6:7-8

13

HELP ME OPEN HEART AND HOME, LORD

I was moved last night
when my friend of many years said artlessly,
"My heart has grown too big to turn away any
    children."
She wasn't bragging, Lord.
She was simply stating a truth:
She who has taken
the psychologically and spiritually poor
into her home for over twenty years
can always find room for one more.

As I waited for dinner, I watched
the remarried and single moms
trek in to claim their peaceful children.
For years my friend has provided
after-school care for children
of divorce without charge.
At her place they receive art lessons,
pony rides, homemade bread, nurture.

Said one single mother of a six-year-old son,
"She is mother of us all."

Moreover,
she and her husband, a country doctor,
house three European students,
an unmarried doctor who's waiting for a house,
and three of their five children under one roof.
In addition, she has "adopted" a single mom
and her three-year-old and cares for both.

What sweet peace was in that place!
I could almost feel your blessing resting upon
this family that has shared their home,
their lives, their food, with others over the years.
They believe, Lord, that's what Christianity is
    all about.
They say they are simply imitating you.

I have lived otherwise:
        Self-protective, eager to live the writer's life,
        I have nurtured my own but have not always
            opened my home
            to those in need.

Forgive me, Lord.
Help me start anew—
to take seriously James's sobering words:
Religion that God our Father
accepts as pure and faultless is this:
to look after orphans and widows in their distress
and to keep oneself from being
polluted by the world.

What more do you desire from me, Lord?

"Is not this the kind of fasting I have chosen:
to loose the chains of injustice
and untie the cords of the yoke,
to set the oppressed free
and break every yoke?
Is it not to share your food with the hungry
and to provide the poor wanderer with shelter—
when you see the naked, to clothe him,
and not to turn away from your own flesh and blood?

"Then your light will break forth like the dawn,
and your healing will quickly appear;
then your righteousness will go before you,
and the glory of the LORD will be your rear guard.
Then you will call, and the LORD will answer;
you will cry for help and he will say, Here am I."

O Father, help me to have an open home
and a responsive heart.
To genuinely care about social justice and the poor.

Give me a new heart so that
I, like my friend, may someday say,
"My heart has grown too big
to turn anyone away."

JAMES 1:27, ISAIAH 58:6-9

He who is kind to the poor lends to the LORD,
and he will reward him for what he has done.

PROVERBS 19:17

If anyone has material possessions and sees his brother
in need but has no pity on him, how can the love of
God be in him?

1 JOHN 3:17

14

I'M WORRIED ABOUT MONEY JUST NOW, LORD

As I look ahead, I wonder
how we will pay the bills,
take care of an ailing parent,
fund the children's needs,
and have something left over
for clothes and simple pleasures.

How can my husband and I possibly have enough
to hedge against the high cost
of a life-threatening illness, health insurance,
or the expense of growing old?

Even though we tithe,
the unexpected large expense
still sends shock waves through my system, Lord.
When the car dies, or sewer lines get clogged
and a backhoe must dig up the lawn,
or when we hear we must replace
our old, rusty furnace,
my anxiety level skyrockets.

Yet when I look back over my life,
I see that you have always taken care of us.
We have never missed a meal or been homeless.
Even as a single mother,
I was able to work from home part-time,
available to my children.
You supplied our needs. Always.

Thank you for reminding me
that I must fight my natural anxiety about money.
Your Word says:
Keep your lives free
from the love of money and
be content with what you have
because God has said,
"Never will I leave you;
never will I forsake you."

Help me, like the apostle Paul, to be content
whatever my circumstances,
whether experiencing poverty or plenty,
for everything I have comes from you.
And help me never to try to keep up with the Joneses.
The Joneses have only gotten richer over the years!
And Lord, may I not waste another precious hour
on earth worrying about things
you have promised will come to me
as a matter of course if I will put my entire focus
    on you:

Food, clothes, and even life itself
will flow toward me if I seek you first.
Thank you, Father.
You will give me all that I need for today
and any tomorrows you have allotted for me.

HEBREWS 13:5; PHILIPPIANS 4:11-13;
MATTHEW 6:25-27,33-34

Then Jesus said to his disciples:
"Therefore I tell you, do not worry
about your life, what you will eat;
or about your body, what you will wear.
Life is more than food, and the body more than clothes.
Consider the ravens: They do not sow or reap,
they have no storeroom or barn; yet God feeds them.
And how much more valuable are you than birds!"

LUKE 12:22-24

15

HOW CAN I POSSIBLY LOVE
THE OTHER WOMAN, LORD?

How can I love the other woman who invaded
    my first marriage?
How can any of us
love those who have torn our hearts asunder—
        abusive parents,
            cheating spouses,
                dishonest business partners,
                    unfaithful friends?

How the heart burns when betrayed!
Rejected by those
who were supposed to love us—
we rehearse the wrongs to all
who will listen.
We lie awake during sleepless nights,
remembering, hurting, fretting, plotting.
Ah, but the feelings run deep, Lord.

You know that sometimes in the deepest night
I compose letters in my mind to those who have
    wronged me.

How I struggle to forgive my ancient enemies—
my ex-husband and the woman
he had an affair with and later married.
The pain my children have experienced at his hand
makes total forgiveness hard.

Love him and the woman
who left her husband to claim mine?

How can I possibly do this, Lord?
You ask too much.

Yet your Word refuses to let me off the hook:
"You have heard that it was said,
'Love your neighbor and hate your enemy.'
But I tell you: Love your enemies and
pray for those who persecute you,
that you may be sons of your Father in heaven.
He causes his sun to rise on the evil and the good,
and sends rain on the righteous and the unrighteous.
If you love those who love you,
what reward will you get?
Are not even the tax collectors doing that?
And if you greet only your brothers,
what are you doing more than others?
Do not even pagans do that?

"Be perfect, therefore, as your heavenly Father is perfect."

That's a tough standard, Lord.
Help me to do the impossible—
   to let go of any injuries and forgive,
   to feed my hungry enemy,
   to quench his thirst,
   to overcome evil with good.

Only with the help of your Holy Spirit
can I ever do this.
I want to obey you, Lord, I do.
I know I'd sleep better and
my body would experience less tension.
Help me release these
toxins of the soul and spirit.
Cleanse my heart for Jesus' sake.
Please set me free.

MATTHEW 5:43-48, ROMANS 12:19-21

If your enemy is hungry, give him food to eat;
if he is thirsty, give him water to drink.
In doing this, you will heap burning coals
on his head, and the LORD will reward you.

PROVERBS 25:21-22

16

LORD, HOW HEALING NATURE CAN BE

What a gift you have given us in the world we inhabit!
How often I go through my days, unconscious of
nature's nurturing backdrop in my life!

Thank you, Father, for bringing me to this place
    apart,
this retreat hidden in deep forest
where you are healing and restoring my soul.
How we women need this;
we, the emotional caretakers
for family and friends,
must recover solitude in order to
        think
        listen
        simply *be*.
How we need uninterrupted hours
to range through your Word.
Asking questions.
Listening.
Feeling your nearness.

Months ago I cried out to you, saying
I desperately needed to get away alone.
You heard.
You responded,
bringing me to this lovely place
to renew my hope in you and
sharpen my senses.

As I sit at this weathered table, barefoot,
my senses are coming alive as never before.
Your world has never seemed more immediate or
    beautiful.
Instead of the distant roar of traffic and planes
flying overhead, I hear soft sounds.
      A distant bird call.
      A fly buzzing.
      The faint barking of a dog.
And your sun!
As I sit outside in a canvas chair,
I feel summer invade every cell of my body,
bathing me in tranquillity.
Down the hill is a wildflower garden
full of reds, yellows, pinks.
Along its edge is a row of huge, succulent blackberries
without thorns.

Truly, the heavens declare your glory,
and the skies proclaim the work of your hands!
Day after day they pour forth speech;

night after night they display knowledge.
There is no speech or language
where their voice is not heard.
Their voice goes out into all the earth,
their words to the ends of the world.

Lord, you created our marvelous world
in the beginning of time
while the morning stars sang together
and all the angels shouted for joy.
And after you had created the heavens, the
earth, the animals, and the vegetation,
you said that it was good.
And it is.
So very good.

How grateful I am that you care deeply about the
       natural world.
You told Job that you satisfy the lion's hunger
and feed the hungry ravens.
You even track the mountain goats and
know when they give birth.
O Father, if you have such concern for the animals
you created,
surely you have concern for me.
Nature is not here by accident.
Nor am I.
Thank you for the wonder of this place.
For the glorious world you have called into being.

Thank you that today I can partake of the
healing therapy that is nature.
And when I must pack my bags and return home,
will you go with me?

*"You will go out in joy and be led forth in peace;
the mountains and hills will burst into song
before you, and all the trees of the field will
clap their hands. Instead of the thornbush
will grow the pine tree, and instead of briers
the myrtle will grow."*

PSALM 19:1-4, JOB 38:7, GENESIS 1:1-31, JOB 38:39–39:2,
ISAIAH 55:12-13

*"Who provides food for the raven when its young
cry out to God and wander about for lack of food?
Do you know when the mountain goats give birth?
Do you watch when the doe bears her fawn?
Do you count the months till they bear?
Do you know the time they give birth?"*

JOB 38:41–39:2

17

TODAY I FEEL WEAK
AND INVISIBLE

When I look in the mirror, I see
a person of little influence and personal power,
yet I live in a city where power and influence are
    everything.
Everywhere I go I'm commanded
to be rich and thin and beautiful.
And young.
Always young.
But I have never been rich or terribly thin or
    beautiful,
nor do thousands flock to hear me speak;
my name isn't a household word.
I have never had the proverbial fifteen minutes
of fame and glory.

How grateful I am, O Lord,
that you seldom call the rich, the wise,
the powerful, the beautiful.
Indeed, you do just the opposite.

The apostle Paul told the Corinthians:

Not many of you were wise
by human standards;
not many were influential;
not many were of noble birth.

Instead, you chose the foolish things
of the world to shame the wise;
you *chose the weak things*
of the world
to shame the strong.

And why, O Lord,
did you choose the lowly and despised?
So that none could boast
about himself or his accomplishments
in your presence.

Even Christ's disciples were a
disappointing group of recruits.
A motley, ragtag assortment of humans.
To a man, all denied Christ in his loneliest hour.
And yet, after his resurrection,
the weak and disloyal suddenly became the bold
        and courageous.

Lord, work your alchemy in me
just as you changed Jesus' disciples.
Transform me
        through the power of Christ's resurrection.

So that, though I am weak and broken and small,
    I may prove useful in your hands.

How I long to do something lasting for your
    kingdom, Lord.
As I wait for your life-changing power,
thank you that it's okay to be me.

            1 CORINTHIANS 1:26-29

*But he said to me, "My grace is sufficient for you,
for my power is made perfect in weakness." Therefore
I will boast all the more gladly about my weaknesses,
so that Christ's power may rest on me.*

            2 CORINTHIANS 12:9

18

LORD, I DON'T KNOW WHAT TO DO...

I'm scared, Father,
struggling about which way to go.
Before me lie two roads, shrouded in mist.
I am not sure which one to take.
What if I choose the wrong one?
The consequences could shatter my life.

Please help me, Lord.
How I long for some visible sign of your guidance.
How I wish I could hear your voice saying,
    "This is the road to take."
You guided the ancient Israelites with a cloud
    by day
and a fiery orb by night.

But I have no cloud to guide me.
So how can I be certain which road to take?

I'm grateful your Word tells me:
Whether you turn to the right or
to the left, your ears will hear

a voice behind you, saying,
"This is the way; walk in it."
I will instruct you and teach you
in the way you should go;
I will counsel you and watch over you.
Do not be like the horse or the mule,
which have no understanding
but must be controlled by bit and bridle
or they will not come to you.
Many are the woes of the wicked,
but the LORD's unfailing love
surrounds the man who trusts in him.

Thank you, Father, that I am not alone
in this difficult situation.

If any of you lacks wisdom,
he should ask God, who gives generously
to all without finding fault, and
it will be given him.

Help me to believe the answer is on the way.
Help me not to doubt.
I have been like the waves of the sea,
tossed about by the winds of opinion.
Forgive my double-mindedness.
Even though I have no visible cloud to guide me,
I have someone better—
        your counselor, the Holy Spirit.

He will guide and instruct me in
all the decisions of my life.
This comforts me, Lord.
My eyes are upon you.

NUMBERS 9:15-17, ISAIAH 30:21, PSALM 32:8-10,
JAMES 1:5-8, JOHN 16:13

*"I have much more to say to you,
more than you can now bear.
But when he, the Spirit of truth, comes,
he will guide you into all truth."*

JOHN 16:12-13

19

TAME MY TONGUE, LORD

Last night my husband and I had an argument.
I said things I regret. He did too.
I felt he didn't hear me;
he felt I misunderstood his intentions.
Today both of us are wounded, unable to
        communicate
from our deepest hearts.
Our problem remains unresolved.
As he left for work, I realized anew that words
convey both life and death;
They build up and tear down—
within the space of a few moments.

As James said, no one can tame the tongue;
though it's a small part of the body,
it's a fire that corrupts and
sets entire lives ablaze.

Since I cannot tame my tongue, O Father,
I submit it and all my words to you.
Change me, Lord.

Help me to become the wife my husband needs,
to respect his person and position in my life and
to appreciate his myriad good deeds
        instead of focusing on the things he fails to do.
Help me to accept him as he is
        instead of attempting to remake him in my
                image,
to remember his daily acts of sacrificial love.

I long to imitate
the wife of noble character in Proverbs,
who brings her husband good, not harm,
all the days of her life.

I know I have failed at times to be the wife
my husband needs,
yet he always forgives.
This man never holds grudges.
In that respect, he is like you.

Please remake me, Lord, from the inside out.
Let my words be gentle and
my mouth become a fountain of life.
Help me to praise you in all the
moments of my marriage—
the good times and the bad.

*"I live in a high and holy place,
but also with him who is contrite and lowly in spirit,*

*to revive the spirit of the lowly
and to revive the heart of the contrite."*

JAMES 3:5-8; EPHESIANS 5:33; PROVERBS 31:10,12; 10:11;
ISAIAH 57:15

*When words are many, sin is not absent, but he
who holds his tongue is wise. The tongue of the
righteous is choice silver, but the heart of the
wicked is of little value.*

PROVERBS 10:19-20

*Reckless words pierce like a sword,
but the tongue of the wise brings healing.*

PROVERBS 12:18

21

THANK YOU, LORD, FOR THIS WONDERFUL GRANDBABY

How I live for my grandbaby's smells and coos!
When I hold him and listen to his regular breathing as
he sleeps peacefully in my arms,
my heart sings.
I praise you for his life.
What an amazing God you are to have
formed his little body
in the secret place of his mother's womb.
Tiny fingers and toes,
rosebud mouth,
long eyelashes.
How I love your attention to detail!

Thank you, Father, for our babies and grandbabies,
for the privilege of nurturing each new generation
and teaching each child about your love and power.
For the healing we find as we nurture our babies
   and grandbabies
      in ways we were never nurtured,
      becoming the mothers and grandmothers we
         never had—
      but always wanted.

Today an unmothered friend said,
"When I hold this grandchild,
feelings of fulfillment start at my head and go down
to my toes. It's as if my painful childhood never was."

You knew that each baby would become
    a symbol of hope,
signifying the dawning of a new day.
The psalmist said,
From the lips of children and infants
you have ordained praise.
How wonderful that our babies and grandchildren
can praise you.

When I hold my grandson—
so fresh and green—
I whisper in his tiny ear that I love him
and that you, dear Father, have sent him
during this difficult time
        to lift my heart,
          to give me hours of pleasure,
            to inspire me to live long enough
               to watch him stride into manhood.
Thank you, Father, for this gift-child,
so perfectly timed in his parents' lives and in mine.
What joy he brings!

PSALM 139:13, 8:2

Sons are a heritage from the LORD,
children a reward from him.
Like arrows in the hands of a warrior
are sons born in one's youth.
Blessed is the man whose quiver is full of them.
They will not be put to shame
when they contend with their enemies in the gate.

PSALM 127:3-5

21

LORD, I AM LONELY TODAY

Summer wanes.
The whole world, it seems,
is on vacation.
My friends have fled the city
for mountains, lakes, and beaches.
And I am home.
Alone.
I wander through the house, restless,
longing for some good hours with
an understanding friend.

I confess, Lord,
that I sometimes feel ashamed when I am lonely—
thinking something is wrong with me
since I am unable to constantly surround myself
    with friends.

Thank you for reminding me that in feeling lonely,
I am part of struggling humanity.
How lonely Job must have felt when his
well-meaning comforters
blamed him for his own suffering.

Job cried out,
"A despairing man
should have the devotion of his friends...
but my brothers are as undependable
as intermittent streams."

At the end of his life,
the apostle Paul felt abandoned and alone.
He wrote:
At my first defense, no one came to my support,
but everyone deserted me.
May it not be held against them.
But the Lord stood at my side and
gave me strength, so that through me
the message might be fully
proclaimed and all the Gentiles
might hear it.

Even your Son experienced a
desperate kind of loneliness
in Gethsemane.
His insensitive disciples fell sleep
in his darkest hour—though
he'd asked them to pray with him.
"Could you men not keep watch
with me for one hour?" Christ asked.
Later he said, *"Are you still sleeping and resting?*
Look, the hour is near, and the Son of Man
is betrayed into the hands of sinners."

O what depths of human loneliness
Christ must have experienced in Gethsemane
   and on the cross!
Surely he understands and
empathizes with my pain.

Thank you, Lord, for sending your son
to identify with my human condition.
Thank you, Father, for the
sweetness of your presence and your
assurance that you will never
desert me, no matter what I face in life.

"Though the mountains be shaken and
the hills be removed,
yet my unfailing love for you
will not be shaken
nor my covenant of peace be removed,"
says the LORD, who has compassion on you.

JOB 6:14-15, 2 TIMOTHY 4:16-17, MATTHEW 26:36-45,

ISAIAH 54:10

"And surely I am with you always,
to the very end of the age."

MATTHEW 28:20

22

FREE ME FROM SHAME, LORD

On one level, I've probably felt some sense of shame
all my life—
> ashamed of my early neediness and
> > dependency,
> of emotional needs my parents could not
> > meet.
> Then came the divorce and the humiliation
> of the other woman.
When I sin knowingly,
I feel ashamed.
I feel a dissonance between
> the kind of person I want to be,
> > the person others think I am,
> > > and the woman I truly am.

I work hard to create
this persona, Lord.
Who wants the world to listen
in on her marital quarrels?
Her snarls at the kids?
What woman alive wants
her secret thoughts broadcast over the airwaves?

But you know the deepest
recesses of my heart.
You know who I *really* am—
        and STILL you love me.

It comforts me that David,
a king and man after your own heart,
also wrestled with shame.
He wrote:
Remember not the sins of my youth
and my rebellious ways;
according to your love remember me,
for you are good, O LORD.
No one whose hope is in you
will ever be put to shame.

Father, thank you that I can come
to you with all my neediness and all those
        uncomfortable feelings of dependency.
You alone are the parent who can
meet all of my emotional needs.
And you never make me
feel ashamed.
Instead, you whisper, "I love you."
You tell me,
"Do not be afraid; you will not suffer shame.
Do not fear disgrace; you will not be humiliated.
You will forget the shame of your youth
and remember no more the reproach of your
        widowhood.

Though the mountains be shaken
and the hills be removed,
yet my unfailing love for you will not be shaken
nor my covenant of peace be removed."

PSALM 25:7,3; ISAIAH 54:4,10

Those who look to him are radiant;
their faces are never covered with shame.

PSALM 34:5

23

HELP ME FACE THIS
LIFE-THREATENING ILLNESS

How glad I am to be alive today, Lord—
      to feel the sunshine warming my back,
      to hear the rustling of leaves in the forest,
         the persistent buzz of insects.
In this illness you are teaching me
      not to take life and health and breath for
      granted.

Yet—
I yearn
to grow old with my husband,
to become an old woman
who will smile on her great-grandchildren.
Like Hezekiah, I cry out to you,
sometimes weeping bitterly
as I plead for additional years.
If you heal me, I will, like Hezekiah,
walk humbly all my years
because of this anguish of my soul.
Like Hezekiah, I wish to say,
Surely it was for my benefit
that I suffered such anguish.

O Lord, you added fifteen years
to Hezekiah's life.
Will you spare mine?

"I have loved you with an everlasting love;
I have drawn you with loving-kindness.
I will build you up again
and you will be rebuilt, O Virgin Israel.
Again you will take up your tambourines
and go out to dance with the joyful.
I will turn their mourning into gladness;
I will give them comfort and joy instead of sorrow.

"For I know the plans I have for you,…
plans to prosper you and not to harm you,
plans to give you hope and a future.

"I will restore you to health
and heal your wounds."

ISAIAH 38:15,17,5; JEREMIAH 31:3-4,13; 29:11; 30:17

Heal me, O LORD, and I will be healed;
save me and I will be saved, for
you are the one I praise.

JEREMIAH 17:14

But he was pierced for our transgressions,
he was crushed for our iniquities;
the punishment that brought us peace was upon him,
and by his wounds we are healed.

ISAIAH 53:5

24

TODAY, GOD, I'M STRUGGLING TO BE HOSPITABLE

Friends just called,
wanting to come and stay for several days.
All I can think about is the
time and energy it will take to clean this house,
shop for food, and fix the meals.
I feel tired and pressed just now, Lord.
My tendency is to put them off,
to wait for another time—
a better, freer time.

But something stopped
me from saying no.
Was it the memory of the satisfying feeling
I usually get when I look down
our old pine table and see my
husband, children, and friends of many years
laughing and talking together?

We've had young children together,
attended graduations and weddings,
and now I'm getting to know their
adult children.

Thank you, Lord, for bringing
these dear friends into my life
and keeping them there.
As I prepare my home, will you
prepare my heart?

Thank you for reminding me that
Jesus took hospitality seriously and
he urged us to host a banquet and
invite those who could not reciprocate:
the poor, the crippled, the lame, the blind.
He promised blessings if we obeyed.
Perhaps he did this, in part,
for those like me who think in terms
of payback.

Your Word tells us to *offer hospitality
to one another without grumbling,*
to *not forget to entertain strangers,
for by so doing some people
have entertained angels
without knowing it.*

Father, thank you for these gentle admonitions.
Help me to remember all those
who have been hospitable to me and
my family across the years.

Help me to do for them
what they have so graciously

done for me and mine.
Help me to make these beds, clean this house,
and prepare these meals—
all for the love of Jesus and
in the name of friendship.

I feel better already, Lord.

LUKE 14:12-14, 1 PETER 4:9, HEBREWS 13:2

A generous man will prosper;
he who refreshes others will himself
be refreshed.

PROVERBS 11:25

Do not eat the food of a stingy man, do
not crave his delicacies; for he is the kind
of man who is always thinking about the cost.
"Eat and drink," he says to you, but his heart
is not with you.

PROVERBS 23:6-7

25

HELP ME NOT
TO JUDGE OTHERS, LORD

I have judged my new friend wrongly.
She said something yesterday that tapped
into my insecurity;
I responded with fierce competitiveness.
Troubled by what she said and by
my own reaction, I didn't come to you.
Instead I talked to another friend about her.

I gossiped, Lord.
Yet even as I did, something inside me
twisted and turned.
I knew I had
wounded the Holy Spirit.

Now I discover I was wrong in
my judgment.
I projected onto her
some of the darkness from my own soul.
She is better, truer than I thought.
When she reached out to me today,
I felt ashamed.

Your Word also rebuked me:
"Do not judge, or you too will be judged.
For in the same way you judge others,
you will be judged,
and with the measure you use,
it will be measured to you.

"Why do you look at the speck of sawdust
in your brother's eye and pay no attention
to the plank in your own eye?"

Forgive me, Lord,
     for the insecurity and ambition
     that fuel my fierce competitiveness,
     for my propensity to gossip and
     pull another down to my own level.

Help me today to refrain from gossip altogether—
and to think of others as better than myself.
Help me, Lord, to love those who threaten me,
as I try to understand just who they truly are,
and to stand in their shoes.
Finally, Lord, empower me to replace
judgment with kindness, mercy, and love.

MATTHEW 7:1-3

Love is patient, love is kind. It does not envy,
it does not boast, it is not proud. It is not rude,
it is not self-seeking, it is not easily angered,
it keeps no record of wrongs.
Love does not delight in evil,
but rejoices with the truth.
It always protects, always trusts, always hopes,
always perseveres.

1 CORINTHIANS 13:4-7

26

KRISTEN'S SONG: THANK YOU, LORD, FOR THE JOYS OF MOTHERHOOD

What a delight this baby is!
How I love his gurgles and laughter,
his wet kisses as he grabs
my face in his hands.
His squeals of glee as he
paddles his legs in the bathtub,
spraying water over me and all his toys.
What intense love I feel for him—
particularly during those moments
as he lies quietly in my arms,
nursing at my breast
then reaching for my face
to rub noses with me.
How passionate I am about
my child. I want to protect him
from pain or harm.
Is that how you feel about me, Lord?

The prophet Zephaniah says:
"Sing, O Daughter of Zion;
shout aloud, O Israel!
Be glad and rejoice with all your heart....

The LORD, the King of Israel, is with you;
never again will you fear any harm....
The LORD your God is with you,
he is mighty to save.
He will take great delight in you,
he will quiet you with his love,
he will rejoice over you with singing."

Thank you for these promises and for this baby,
    Lord.
He anchors me to life
and captures me in the here and now.
His needs are so immediate,
his love for me so uncomplicated.
He prefers me to all others. Always.
What mother would knowingly give up that place
of unrivaled affection in her child's heart?

As much as I complain
when he awakens me from a sound sleep,
I cherish those moments in the darkness,
holding his limp, sleepy body against mine,
kissing his soft, plump cheeks
flushed red with sleep.
His hand lies still on my shoulder,
and I can hear his measured,
even breathing through
his slightly parted lips.
So content.

So trusting.
So utterly dependent.

Is that how you want me to be, Lord—
totally abandoned to you,
every muscle relaxed in the safety
of your embrace?

Thank you for showing me
through this helpless baby
how you see and love me.
May this baby be a daily reminder
of your power,
your trustworthiness,
your constant and tender love.

ZEPHANIAH 3:14-17

"When they see among them their children,
the work of my hands, they will keep my name holy;
they will acknowledge the holiness of the
Holy One of Jacob, and will stand in awe
of the God of Israel."

ISAIAH 29:23

(Written by my younger daughter, Kristen, just months after
she became a mother for the first time.)

27

THANK YOU FOR FRIENDSHIP, LORD

My friend is struggling, Lord.
She's weary from meeting
the needs of all the people in her life.
Loss makes her heart ache.

I listen,
>   trying to validate her feelings,
>   just as she, on countless other occasions,
>   has listened to me.
>   Long ago we stopped trying
>   to fix each other or solve
>   each other's problems.

When she needed to go,
we prayed.
How many prayers
have we offered for our
husbands, children, others over the years?
How many times have I listened
to her pray for me and felt
nurtured and even healed?

Lord, I love this friend
you have placed in my life.
She never drags me down.
Even when she speaks the hard truth,
she is *a friend who sticks closer*
than a brother.
As iron sharpens iron,
so we sharpen each other.

She and I have learned across the years
       to ask for forgiveness and
       to trust each other
       with our vulnerable selves.

She comforts me when I'm heartsore;
I do the same for her.
We confess our sins without shame,
knowing we will not be judged.
And we always laugh.
Sometimes even through tears.

Lately, we've begun to talk
of growing old together, two gray-haired women,
historians of each other's lives.

My friend is a gift from you, Lord.
Only you knew that we could learn
to walk together in such synchrony and joy.
Consciously we work to keep you at the center of
       our relationship.

Thank you, Lord, for inventing friendship and
for giving us those wonderful role models:
        Jonathan and David,
        Ruth and Naomi,
        Jesus with Mary, Martha, and Lazarus.

You understand our need for
intimate bonds with our true friends
as well as family.
Bless my friend today, Lord.
Give her comfort.
Give her wings.

PROVERBS 18:24, 27:17

Two are better than one....
If one falls down, his friend can help
him up. But pity the man who falls
and has no one to help him up!

ECCLESIASTES 4:9-10

28

I FEEL CONDEMNED, LORD

Sometimes I feel
as if I stand before a judge—myself—
and hear the pounding of the gavel,
along with these piercing words:
>"You have not been the person
>you were meant to be.
>Instead of thirsting for God,
>you have pursued fun, toys,
>success, accomplishment."

What angst I feel at such times as I remember things
      I've said
      and done that have hurt others,
      as well as myself.

How I want to be more than I am, Lord.
How I want you
to be pleased with me.

But even as my heart condemns me, Father,
I feel the comfort of your presence
and hear these quiet words in

the inner recesses of my being:
"Stop this nonsense."

I run to your Word. I read:
The LORD is compassionate and gracious,
slow to anger, abounding in love.
He will not always accuse,
nor will he harbor his anger forever;
he does not treat us as our sins deserve
or repay us according to our iniquities.
For as high as the heavens are above the earth,
so great is his love for those who fear him;
as far as the east is from the west,
so far has he removed our transgressions from us.

And when I fear that Christ will condemn me?

There is now no condemnation
for those who are in Christ Jesus,
because through Jesus Christ
the law of the Spirit of life set me free
from the law of sin and death.

Thank you, Lord, for saving me—
from my sins and from myself.
I never need
to feel condemned again.

And when I sin anew,
as I surely will today?

I have only to run to you
and openly confess the darkness
in my human heart.
You are *faithful and just and will forgive us
our sins and purify us from all unrighteousness.*

Praise you, Lord.
What a relief to know I no longer need to
drag a ball and chain behind me.
I am free—at last.

PSALM 103:8-12, ROMANS 8:1-2, 1 JOHN 1:9

*Therefore, if anyone is in Christ, he is a
new creation; the old has gone, the new
has come!*

2 CORINTHIANS 5:17

29

I'M WORRYING AGAIN, LORD

The worry habit is so
ingrained and unconscious
that before I know it,
I have wasted precious minutes—hours—
worrying about *what if.*
>   *What if* we can't pay all our
>   bills in the future?
>   *What if* my child isn't
>   accepted into the college
>   of his choice?
>   *What if* my marriage falters?
>   *What if* I lose this friendship?
>   *What if* I lose my health entirely?

How can I break the worry habit, Lord?
How can I learn to live with
peace and joy and gratitude
in the moment?

I hear these words in my heart:
Do not be anxious about anything,

but in everything, by prayer and petition,
with thanksgiving,
present your requests to God.
And the peace of God, which transcends
all understanding,
will guard your hearts and your minds
in Christ Jesus.

What comfort these words are, Lord.
And if that is not enough to
break the worry habit,
then I will meditate on Christ's
liberating words:
"Who of you by worrying
can add a single hour to his life?
Since you cannot do this very little thing,
why do you worry about the rest?"

Why indeed!
I get the message, Lord.
Thank you.

Philippians 4:6-7, Luke 12:25-26

"Do not be afraid, little flock, for your Father
has been pleased to give you the kingdom.
Sell your possessions and give to the poor.
Provide purses for yourselves that will not wear out,

a treasure in heaven that will not be exhausted,
where no thief comes near and no moth destroys.
For where your treasure is, there your heart will be also."

LUKE 12:32-34

30

HELP ME, FATHER, TO BECOME
A GENEROUS GIVER

I confess I haven't
spent time lately
thinking about giving.
Nor do I directly care for the poor
as I live my insulated life in suburbia.
And I am sometimes slow
in bringing my full
tithe to your house.

I wince inside when I admit this, Lord—
I am robbing you!
Yet when I do give,
all too often I do so dutifully,
not cheerfully.
Forgive me, Lord.
Give me a new heart—
        a heart of flesh for this heart of stone.

I have been poor,
        utterly dependent on you
        for bread and clothes and jobs.

I then bridled at the stinginess
and insensitivity of the rich.
Have I now become one of them?

Whoever sows sparingly
will also reap sparingly,
and whoever sows generously
will also reap generously.
Each man should give what
he has decided in his heart to give,
not reluctantly or under compulsion,
for God loves a cheerful giver.

And if I do this?
Your Word promises that the cheerful giver
will be made rich in every way,
able to be generous on every occasion.
Moreover, all of my generosity
will result in thanksgiving to you.

What a deal!
Help me today to begin giving generously
so that someday I may dance
into your presence—
a cheerful, hilarious giver—
confident that because of my generosity,
others have offered up to you the
sweet incense of grateful prayer.

MALACHI 3:8,6, EZEKIEL 36:26, 2 CORINTHIANS 9:6-11

*"Bring the whole tithe into the storehouse,
that there may be food in my house. Test me in this,"
says the LORD Almighty, "and see if I will
not throw open the floodgates of heaven and
pour out so much blessing that you will not have room
enough for it."*

MALACHI 3:10

31

LORD, MY HUSBAND
NEEDS A CHEERFUL WIFE

Today I want to be a cheerful wife for my husband.
As we teased each other and laughed this morning,
I realized how important it is
to be cheerful and to have a merry heart.
I also saw how encouraged my husband was,
how light his step, as he closed the door
on his way to work.
And as we talked throughout the day,
I could hear the warmth in his voice—
a carryover from our happy exchange this morning.

Help me on other days
to be the cheerful wife my husband needs, Lord—
to provide the peaceful home he yearns for.
There are few things worse
than an argumentative wife spoiling for a fight.
Proverbs says it well:
Better to live on a corner of the roof
than share a house with a quarrelsome wife.
Better to live in a desert
than with a quarrelsome and ill-tempered wife.

There are some days, I'm sure, when my husband
longs to flee to a rooftop
or to a faraway desert to find restoration and peace—
days when I'm anything but peaceful.

Father, help me to create
a safe place for him to be truly at home.
A place where he can be renewed and
gain strength to go out and conquer
the giants in the workplace.
A place where he can experience true love
and genuine respect.

With your help, Father, I can become the wife who
    makes that happen.

PROVERBS 21:9,19

A quarrelsome wife is like a constant dripping
on a rainy day; restraining her is like
restraining the wind or grasping oil with the hand.

PROVERBS 27:15-16

32

O FATHER, I'VE COME TO THE END
OF MY TETHER

Like Paul in ancient Asia,
I am under great pressure,
    carrying a load heavier
    than I can possibly bear.
Like this giant of the faith,
I despair and feel in my heart
the sentence of death.
Why have I come to this place, Lord?
And what am I to do?

Perhaps I am experiencing this hardship
so that I, like the apostle Paul,
can learn to rely completely on you
and not on my feeble, human self.
You can deliver me from this perilous
place, just as you delivered Paul.
And you can keep on delivering me
all the days of my life,
bringing me safely into your heavenly kingdom.

Thank you that you are
the God of all comfort

who comforts us in all our troubles,
so that we can comfort those
in any trouble with the comfort
we ourselves have received from God.

Thank you that
just as the sufferings of Christ
flow over into our lives,
so also through Christ our comfort overflows.

How I need your comfort just now, Lord.
You are all I have for sure.
I will rely on you alone.

2 CORINTHIANS 1:8-10,3-5

In this you greatly rejoice, though now for a little while
you may have had to suffer grief in all kinds of trials.
These have come so that your faith—of greater worth
than gold, which perishes even though refined by fire—
may be proved genuine and may result in praise,
glory and honor when Jesus Christ is revealed.

1 PETER 1:6-7

33

LORD, PLEASE SEND SOMEONE
TO WATCH OVER ME

Lord, I long for someone to
watch over me—
> someone a few steps ahead
> who can pull me up to the next rock
> as we climb together this
> mountain called life.

Father, I need a wise, older woman to
instruct me in how to nurture
my sometimes irascible children—
someone to encourage me,
to normalize my maternal feelings,
someone to keep me hoping when
my husband and I are estranged.

I look for her in Bible studies
and at church—all the right places.
But where is she?
The older women I know are
busy with their own families
or careers.

Lord, I desperately need this
older friend—this mentor—
to laugh with, talk to, pray with.

When I go to your Word,
I am encouraged by the
relationship Ruth had
with her mother-in-law, Naomi.
They shared a rare kind of love.
Ruth even said to her mentor:
*"Where you go I will go,
and where you stay I will stay.
Your people will be my people
and your God my God."*

Where would Ruth have been,
after she lost her husband, without
Naomi to mentor her and lead her to Boaz?
And where would bitter Naomi have
been without Ruth's love and hope
anchoring her to Earth?
Ruth even made Naomi a grandmother!

O Father, you obviously understand.
But what am I to do with my hunger
for this mentoring relationship?

*"Whatever you ask for in prayer,
believe that you have received it,
and it will be yours."*

I am praying.
I am believing.
I am waiting.

RUTH 1:16, MARK 11:24

*Likewise, teach the older women to be reverent in the
way they live, not to be slanderers or addicted to much
wine, but to teach what is good. Then they can train
the younger women to love their husbands and children,
to be self-controlled and pure, to be busy at home,
to be kind, and to be subject to their husbands, so that
no one will malign the word of God.*

TITUS 2:3-5

34

I'M ANXIOUS TODAY, FATHER

The sky is about to fall
on this Chicken Little.
Why am I so restless and jumpy—
disquieted in my soul?

I don't know, Lord.
Maybe it's because of trying to live up to
       other people's expectations,
       my own internal pressures,
       or maybe I'm reeling from
       those nasty hormones.

Lord, whatever is creating this anxiety,
I bring it to you.
You alone have the answers
to my questions.
Only you have the peace
I crave just now.
My soul finds rest in God alone....
He alone is my rock and my salvation;

he is my fortress,
I will never be shaken.

And even though I'm feeling shaky inside,
you will never allow me to be
toppled or destroyed.
I pour out my heart to you.
When I am afraid,
I will trust in you....
In God I trust; I will not be afraid.
What can mortal man do to me?

Your Word assures me that I am your
constant concern and that the love
Christ has for me is
wide and long and high and deep.

Lord,
you will keep in perfect peace
him whose mind is steadfast, because
he trusts in you.

May I be that person today.
No longer Chicken Little,
may I be serene and fearless.

PSALM 62:1-2, 56:3-4, EPHESIANS 3:18, ISAIAH 26:3

I sought the LORD, and he answered me;
he delivered me from all my fears.

PSALM 34:4

The righteous cry out, and the LORD hears them;
he delivers them from all their troubles.

PSALM 34:17

35

IT'S MORNING,
AND I'M BONE-WEARY, LORD

My days are long, action-packed.
As usual, I'm overscheduled,
trying to cram a twenty-eight-hour day
into twenty-four hours.
I race pell-mell from home to office
to the grocery store to children's games.
I'm exhausted...
I need rest!
Yet when I finally come to you and to your Word,
you whisper that it's those who wait on you
who regain their strength.

Isaiah writes:
Even youths grow tired and weary,
and young men stumble and fall;
but those who hope in the LORD
will renew their strength.
They will soar on wings like eagles;
they will run and not grow weary,
they will walk and not be faint.

Thank you, Father, that
in coming to you,
waiting,
resting,
trusting,
I can go from strength to strength
in this pilgrimage called life.

ISAIAH 40:30-31

Blessed are those whose strength
is in you, who have set their hearts
on pilgrimage. As they pass
through the Valley of Baca,
they make it a place of springs;
the autumn rains also cover it with pools.
They go from strength to strength,
till each appears before God in Zion.

PSALM 84:5-7

36

I'm envious, Lord

When I see how you have blessed
my friend this past year,
and compare her good fortune
to my dark gifts of pain,
darkness fills my soul.

Like Joseph's brothers,
I feel that you, Father,
love this friend better than you love me.
But when I tell myself this,
something inside gets twisted and ugly.
The worm turns.

O Father, please banish this enveloping gloom.
I know that envy consumed the hearts
of Joseph's brothers,
prompting them to
sell him into Egypt—
        into servitude, loneliness, sorrow—
        into years of family pain.

Help me, O Lord, to see envy
and selfish ambition as you see it.

James wrote:
But if you harbor
bitter envy and selfish ambition
in your hearts,
do not boast about it or
deny the truth.
Such "wisdom" does not
come down from heaven
but is earthly, unspiritual,
of the devil.
For where you have envy
and selfish ambition,
there you find disorder and
every evil practice.

Forgive me, Lord.
I run to you for cover.
Help me to resist the devil and watch
him flee from me.

The antidote to envy and
selfish ambition is the awareness
that you, O Lord, love me
and have a plan
for my life that is uniquely mine.
My friend is in a happy period

of her life just now and needs me
to be joyful with her.
In time, she will face her own inevitable struggles.

If I keep my eyes focused on you,
I can have some incredibly happy days,
even in rain and snow and sleet.
Suffering does not preclude joy.
Thank you for reminding me of this truth, Lord.

Cleanse me with hyssop,
and I will be clean;
wash me, and I will be
whiter than snow.

GENESIS 37, JAMES 3:14-16, PSALM 51:7

"For I know the plans I have for you,"
declares the LORD, "plans to prosper
you and not to harm you, plans to
give you hope and a future."

JEREMIAH 29:11

37

KEEP ME HOPING, LORD

When what I've
       hoped for,
       prayed for,
       longed for,
       continues to elude me,
I wonder if I will *ever*
have the desires of my heart.
I despair and toy with the idea of securing
for myself that which I long for—
       even if it's second best.
       Even if it might turn
       to ashes in my hand.

It's hard, Lord,
watching you give those
around me their hearts' desires
while I struggle on,
waiting,
praying,
trying to hope.
At such moments, Isaiah's
words ring in my ears:

Who among you fears the LORD
and obeys the word of his servant?
Let him who walks in the dark,
who has no light,
trust in the name of the LORD
and rely on his God.
But now, all you who light fires
and provide yourselves
with flaming torches, go,
walk in the light of your fires
and of the torches you have
set ablaze.
This is what you shall receive
from my hand: You will lie
down in torment.

O Father,
never do I want to follow
my own way and lie down
in torment.
Help my unbelief.

Faith is being sure of
what we hope for and certain
of what we do not see.
Without faith it is impossible to please God,
because anyone who comes to him
must believe that he exists
and that he rewards those
who earnestly seek him.

Father, increase my faith.
Help me to keep coming to you
in the face of unanswered prayer
and years of waiting.
Help me to hope on—
to seek you, the Giver, rather than your gifts
and to believe that because you love me
and do not lie,
I can trust your life-giving words.

ISAIAH 50:10-11; HEBREWS 11:1,6

*Delight yourself in the LORD
and he will give you the desires
of your heart.*

PSALM 37:4

38

Teach me, Father, to truly listen to my child

Teach me to listen to my child, Lord,
when we talk and she tells me
something I don't want to hear—
something that shocks, surprises,
　　　disappoints, or simply catches
　　　me off guard.
When she changes our plans or isn't
enthusiastic about something I propose,
　　　it stings.
At those times, let me hear her needs, not her words:
her fatigue, her difficulty in saying no since
　　　she wants to please,
her desire for personal time and space—
　　　freedom from family,
　　　　　from obligations,
　　　　　　from her mother. (Must I admit it?)

Over the years I have won
battles only to lose later wars.
I know she loves me,
and I dearly love her.
But all our children—though

"gifts and rewards"—belong first
to you and then to themselves.

Thank you, Lord, for this child.
She challenges me to grow
in ways that are uncomfortable to me.
She keeps me stepping up to the plate,
year after year, swinging the bat,
running for first base, second, and third.
But today, Lord, I'm not interested in home runs.
We've had a tussle,
and I need your encouragement.

I know you love my daughter
and are shaping her life and personality
in ways I cannot see.
And as a believer, she deserves
all the respect and forbearance
I would give to any other child of God.

Your Word reminds me:
Honor one another above yourselves.
Live in harmony with one another.
If it is possible, as far as it depends on you,
live at peace with everyone.
And that means our adult children, doesn't it, Lord?

Help me move from a
parent-child relationship to an
adult-adult friendship.

You know this isn't easy, Father.
But we rear our children to let them go.
And though mothers and daughters tend to
remain close throughout life,
I need to step back,
keep quiet on occasion,
and honor my daughter's separateness.
Give me wisdom, Lord.
Help me.

ROMANS 12:10,16,18

Get rid of all bitterness, rage and anger,
brawling and slander, along with every
form of malice. Be kind and compassionate
to one another, forgiving each other,
just as in Christ God forgave you.

EPHESIANS 4:31-32

39

I'M TIRED OF BEING A WIFE AND MOTHER, LORD

Today there are just too many clamorous needs—
  too many meals to prepare,
  too many clothes to mend,
  too many errands to run.
I'm weary of endless carpools,
  dances to chaperone,
  athletic events to attend.
And frankly, the older my
children get, the more thankless
the tasks of parenting seem—
at least some days.
Gone are the days of soft,
cuddly babies, of elementary
school-age children who
adored me.
The heyday of adolescence
has arrived at our house
with its testing,
   testing,
    testing.

My husband and I tumble
into bed at night
too tired to be lovers.
We're weary of holding the line.

Today I long to fly away
to a tropical island.
Alone.
Just to be me again—
whoever that woman is—
and have no one to talk to but you.
To savor sun, sand, ocean,
wind, stars.
Do you understand
my longing, Lord?
You must.
Even Christ retreated at times.

Very early in the morning,
while it was still dark,
Jesus got up, left the house
and went off to a solitary place,
where he prayed.
Simon and his companions
went to look for him,
and when they found him,
they exclaimed, "Everyone is looking for you!"

So Christ, too, needed to be restored
after meeting so many needs.

Help me this day to steal away
in my heart,
to pray and be renewed,
for it's you, Lord, I long for.

O God, you are my God,
earnestly I seek you;
my soul thirsts for you,
my body longs for you,
in a dry and weary land
where there is no water.

Come, Lord,
fill me with your love
so that I can be the wife
and mother you want me to be.

Then I will be "me" in the truest and best sense.

MARK 1:35-37, PSALM 63:1

As the deer pants for streams of water,
so my soul pants for you, O God.
My soul thirsts for God, for the living God.
When can I go to meet with God?

PSALM 42:1-2

40

LORD, I FEEL ANGRY AND REJECTED

My friend has hurt my feelings—again.
Who does she think she is?
Why is she seemingly so
devoid of empathy and understanding?
Has she never suffered?

I know my response is
greater than the situation deserves, but…
I feel rejected when she treats me like this!
She opens old, old wounds
that need your healing touch.
Father, help me sort this out
so I don't internalize anger
and get depressed.

You understand rejection, don't you, Lord?
Not only were you rejected by your
rebellious children, the Israelites,
but your son, Jesus, was no stranger
to the pain of rejection.
He was despised and rejected by men,

a man of sorrows,
and familiar with suffering.
Like one from whom
men hide their faces he was despised,
and we esteemed him not.

Yet even when Christ carried the
weight of the world's rejection,
he took up our infirmities
and carried our sorrows,
the punishment that brought us peace was upon him,
and by his wounds we are healed.

What a Savior! What a Prince of Peace!

O Father, thank you for putting all
my rejections—the old and the new—into
perspective. As painful as they were and are,
I can run to you for healing.

Thank you, Father, that I don't have to
stay in this place of rejection,
but I can bring all my hurts to you,
knowing that no individual
or circumstance can ever separate me
from Christ's love.
In all things
you work for the good of those
who love you.

As for this woman?
She was, after all, only
being thoughtless…human.
Help me to become kind and tender-hearted—
forgiving her as you,
for your son's sake,
have forgiven me.
And help me show her empathy
as I affirm the good gifts she possesses.

Praise you, Father.
I don't have to continue to feel
angry and rejected today.
I can choose how I handle my emotions.
I choose your way.

ISAIAH 53:3-5; ROMANS 8:35-39,28

For I am convinced that neither death nor
life, neither angels nor demons, neither the
present nor the future, nor any powers,
neither height nor depth, nor anything else
in all creation, will be able to separate us from the
love of God that is in Christ Jesus our Lord.

ROMANS 8:38-39

41

I AM AFRAID OF GROWING OLD...

I feel old and unattractive at times, Lord.
I stand in front of the mirror,
examining the crow's feet around my eyes—
      my sagging jowls, my graying,
        thinning hair that the hairdresser
        tries to give a boost with color.
My body doesn't look
like it did ten, even five, years ago.
I've put on weight, and it's moving south.
I don't like to put on a bathing suit anymore,
though I love to go to the beach.

Sometimes I feel my husband
no longer finds me attractive.
He says he does, but
he doesn't take my hand
as often as he once did.
We make love less frequently.
He's aging too,
but men don't seem to agonize
about aging the way we women do.

What can I do, Lord?

I don't want to be
the sad, fiftyish woman
I saw in the mall last night—
with her barrettes, heavy makeup,
bleached-blond hair, and too-short skirt.
Poor soul.
She was a dowager yearning to be a teenybopper.

Since I can't turn back the clock,
how can I grow old gracefully and
accept the inevitable marks of time?

The apostle Peter wrote:
Beauty should not come from outward adornment,
such as braided hair and the
wearing of gold jewelry and fine clothes.
Instead, it should be that of your
inner self, the unfading beauty of a
gentle and quiet spirit,
which is of great worth
in God's sight.

Help me to acquire that quiet and
gentle spirit you value so highly, Lord.
As for gray hair,
rather than cover it up,
help me come to see that
gray hair is *the splendor of the old.*

O Father, may my face, wrinkled though it is,
shine because of the radiance of your presence
so that those who cross my path
will think less of my wrinkles and
more of the warmth of my eyes.
May I, O Lord, be beautiful in you.

1 PETER 3:3-4, PROVERBS 20:29

"Man looks at the outward appearance,
but the LORD looks at the heart."

1 SAMUEL 16:7

42

THANK YOU, LORD, FOR THE JOY OF RECONCILIATION

This morning I read in your Word:
"If you are offering
your gift at the altar and there
remember that your brother has
something against you,
leave your gift there in front of the altar.
First go and be reconciled to your brother; then
come and offer your gift."

Hard words to assimilate, Lord,
but I felt the Holy Spirit's nudging
to call a brother who
wounded me years ago
and ask for his forgiveness
for all the anger and bitterness
I have carried in my heart.

I knew he was still angry at me.

Hesitating briefly, I
quickly dialed his number,

afraid of how he might respond.
When he answered the phone,
I spoke quickly.
"I want to be reconciled with you."
Immediately he said he also
wanted to be reconciled with me.
I cried.
He choked up.
We decided not to run down
our lists of hurts
and misdeeds but rather
to grant each other total forgiveness.

How good it felt, Lord,
when I hung up the phone.
How peaceful I feel now.
How sorry I am that it took me so
many years to obey you.

Thank you for showing me today
that when you tell us, *"Love*
your enemies and pray for
those who persecute you,"
you do so for the good of our souls.

Help me, Lord, to rush to
obey you as you show me
others I need to go to.
I long to hold on to

the shimmering joy
of forgiveness and reconciliation.
I long to feel this free forever.

MATTHEW 5:23-24,44

If anyone says, "I love God," yet hates his brother, he is a liar. For anyone who does not love his brother, whom he has seen, cannot love God, whom he has not seen. And he has given us this command: Whoever loves God must also love his brother.

1 JOHN 4:20-21

43

LORD, MY LIFE FEELS
OUT OF CONTROL

The phone is ringing off the hook.
A friend calls and says she's ill.
As I listen,
I mentally run through the week,
trying to figure out when
I can take her a meal.
My cheerful husband has a day
off work and is looking
for a companion.
A child is needy, and I feel
compelled to hear her out.
Meanwhile, I remember my work deadlines.

What am I to do, Lord?
My stomach is a
tight knot.
I have so many roles—wife,
daughter, friend, mother, worker.
I don't want to race headlong
through my days, failing to listen
to you, stressed to the max.

"In quietness and trust is your strength."

O Father, quiet my heart and
help me entrust this day
and all its demands to you.
How gracious you are when
I cry for help!
Your Word promises
that as soon as you hear,
you will answer.

Help me, Lord, to come to you
at the beginning of my day—
when the house is quiet and
my family sleeps,
to be like the individual described by the psalmist:
*His delight is in the law of the LORD,
and on his law he meditates
day and night.*

Your Word sets me free to
worship you and
surrender all my plans, waiting
for you to show me how to
live this day moment by moment.

Help me, Lord, to seek you
daily and with all my heart,
to hide *your word in my heart
that I might not sin against you.*

#b ct

Start over.

O Father, I desperately need for
you to take control of my life,
to establish my priorities,
teaching me when to say yes
and when to say no.
Help me create healthy boundaries in all my
relationships—
then I can rest in you.

I trust in you, O LORD;
I say, "You are my God."
My times are in your hands.

ISAIAH 30:15,19; PSALM 1:2; 119:10-11; 31:14-15

Praise be to the LORD,
for he showed his wonderful love to me
when I was in a besieged city.

In my alarm I said,
"I am cut off from your sight!"
Yet you heard my cry for mercy
when I called to you for help.

PSALM 31:21-22

44

I HAVE LOVED TEACHING
MY CHILDREN

I have loved teaching my children
about life and about you,
feeling their soft, trusting hands
in mine across the years.
One with the soft cheeks
and compassionate heart,
the other with her well-muscled,
athletic body and great stores of energy.
They are so lovely to me.

I remember cradling them
as babies, holding them
on my lap,
walking beside them on
endless shopping excursions.

I have loved being a mother.
I shall always be grateful
that you took me out of my narcissism
        when you gave me dependent,
            vulnerable children to care for.
As we three have shared simple pleasures—

games, conversations, meals, walks, dreams—
something deep inside has been healed.

I have become the mother I always
wanted to have.

May my husband and I continue to
teach our children
about you, Lord.
May we never trivialize our faith
by our behavior or
our halfhearted obedience.
Help us to love you and
serve you with all our hearts
and souls.

Your Word enjoins parents everywhere to teach
your commandments to their children:

Fix these words of mine in your hearts and minds;
tie them as symbols on your hands and bind
them on your foreheads.

Teach them to your children,
talking about them when you sit at
home and when you walk along the road,
when you lie down and when you get up.

Write them on the doorframes of your houses
and on your gates, so that your days

and the days of your children may be
many in the land that the LORD swore
to give your forefathers, as many as the days
that the heavens are above the earth.

As parents, our lives are those our
children observe and model.
So often, Lord, our children
have stumbled in those same areas
where my husband and I have sinned.

Forgive us, Father.
Purify our hearts
so that you may bless us
in everything
we put our hands to.

DEUTERONOMY 11:18-21, 12:7

These are the commands, decrees and laws
the LORD your God directed me to teach you to
observe in the land that you are crossing
the Jordan to possess, so that you, your children
and their children after them may fear the LORD
your God as long as you live by keeping all his decrees
and commands that I give you, and so that you
may enjoy long life.

DEUTERONOMY 6:1-2

45

IT'S A DREARY DAY, LORD

As I gaze out my window
at the gray day, my heart rebels
at doing all I need to do—
      the dishes, the laundry, the cleaning.
I long to flee to the sun or
      fill my house with light and laughter.
But I have things to do—
      a family to care for and
      promises to keep,
      too many promises to keep.

Are you the Lord of dreary days?
You who made the earth with
all of its elements?
You did not choose to give
us perpetual sunshine
or constant communion with friends.
Instead, you promise
always to give us yourself—
      in sun and in shadow.

Since rebellion never works,
I come to you, Lord,
      relinquishing my plans,
      asking you to banish
      the shadows from my
      mind and heart.

You can change this dreary day
into a wonderful day.
*Put a new song
in my mouth,* O Lord, *a hymn
of praise* to you.
As I sing throughout this house
and my children join in,
make our home
an aviary where our voices lift
heavenward, praising you.

Thank you, Lord, that your Word
contains the antidote for any gray day.
It tells me:
*Speak to one another with psalms,
hymns and spiritual songs.
Sing and make music in
your heart to the Lord,
always giving thanks to
God the Father for everything,
in the name of our Lord Jesus Christ.*

Become the ruler of all my days, Lord—
    the sunny and the gray.
For no matter what the internal
or external weather, I can always choose to
    be grateful.
I can sing and, in the process, grow joyful.
I can always find reasons to praise your holy name.

PSALM 40:3, EPHESIANS 5:19-20

Sing to the LORD a new song;
sing to the LORD, all the earth.
Sing to the LORD, praise his name;
proclaim his salvation day after day.

PSALM 96:1-2

46

WHY DID YOU CREATE ME, LORD?

Sometimes I feel my
life is on cruise control and I'm
dozing at the wheel.
Have I even begun to fulfill
your purposes for me,
to do those good deeds you
planned from the beginning
of time for me to do?
My life is full of
twists and turns,
dead-end streets
and cul-de-sacs.

But wait. I've used the wrong metaphor.

Life is not about highways
and byways.
It's about being clay.
You are the Cosmic Potter, and
I am your clay.

"Like clay in the hand of the potter,
so are you in my hand,
O house of Israel."

You will mold my life—
your pot—
into whatever
shape you choose.

If my life is marred,
you promise to reshape it,
to make it into something
beautiful for you.

Long ago Timothy wrote:
In a large house there are articles not only of
gold and silver, but also of wood and clay;
some are for noble purposes and some for
ignoble. If a man cleanses himself from
the latter, he will be an instrument for
noble purposes, made holy, useful to the
Master and prepared to do any good work.

O Lord, I want to be a
useful, noble vessel in your house.
And yet my life is marred.
Broken.
Will you make my life
beautiful for you?

Will you develop in me
those qualities of love, faith,
        and hope I so desperately need?
I give you my life.

        I give you my heart.
        Help me become pliable,
                simple clay in your competent hands.

JEREMIAH 18:6, 2 TIMOTHY 2:20-21

But just as he who called you is holy,
so be holy in all you do; for it is written:
"Be holy, because I am holy."

1 PETER 1:15-16

47

MY CHILD HAS HURT ME, LORD

Why am I so vulnerable where
my children are concerned, Lord?
Why have I no defenses against
their unkind remarks?
Sometimes they say things that pierce my heart
when they are tired, disgruntled,
or needy
and I am too.
O, how I wish it weren't so.

Then I say words
I deeply regret.
Though we've both
granted each other forgiveness, Lord,
the hurt lingers;
           a black cloud follows wherever I go.

Cruel words are not easily forgotten.

How I have tried to be the
calm, loving, ever-rational mother.

But I have not been able to sustain this.
And as my children have grown,
I've realized that I can help—
but I cannot fix—their problems
or protect them from life's inevitable pain.

Thank you, Lord, for reminding
me that your children also
caused you pain.
You lamented:
"She has not acknowledged
that I was the one who gave
her the grain, the new wine and oil,
who lavished on her the silver
and gold."

And again:
"For a long time I have kept silent,
I have been quiet and held myself back.
But now, like a woman in childbirth,
I cry out, I gasp and pant."

How deeply you care for
us, your children,
even when we wander
and go astray.

And you have implanted that same
parental heart in us:

A longing to have
our children love and not wound us.
A longing to have them
live responsible, godly lives.

O Father, help me accept my
children's humanity.
Just as there are no perfect mothers,
there are no perfect children.
Help me to be the mother
this child needs right now—
    a mother who handles her own life
    with dignity and grace.

And encourage my child to also come to you
in this situation.
Be the bridge between us, Lord,
    teaching her to honor her parent
    while she launches out on her own,
    helping me to ask for forgiveness
    for my hurtful words.
Help us get in touch with
the deep love we feel for each other.
Mother and daughter.
Forever friends.

HOSEA 2:8, ISAIAH 42:14

Hatred stirs up dissension,
but love covers over all wrongs.

PROVERBS 10:12

Dear friends, let us love one another,
for love comes from God. Everyone who loves
has been born of God and knows God....
because God is love.

1 JOHN 4:7-8

48

THIS DECISION IS TOO BIG
FOR ME, LORD

I'm tempted to rely on others
for help in this situation—
to make my decision without
throwing the full weight
of my troubles on you.

Friends urge me to take the
well-worn path, implying that
in seeking you and waiting on
your missive from heaven,
I am doing nothing.

Are they right?

"Woe to the obstinate children,...
to those who carry out plans that are
not mine, forming an alliance,
but not by my Spirit,
heaping sin upon sin;
who go down to Egypt
without consulting me;

who look for help to Pharaoh's protection,
to Egypt's shade for refuge."

Trusting you to lead me, Lord,
is the only course of action that
gives my heart ease.
The path ahead is
uncertain and shrouded in mists.

I have come to you, Lord,
casting myself upon your mercy.
I let go of my trapeze though the
other is barely in sight.
If you don't fling it to me, Lord,
I will crash on the mat below,
a crumpled doll.

But I've been in this place before,
and you've never let me fall.
At points of deepest faith,
life becomes an adventure, and
I sense the full glory of your presence.

Thank you that your Word reminds me
that you always hear and respond:
How gracious he will be when
you cry for help! As soon as he hears,
he will answer you. Although the Lord
gives you the bread of adversity and the water
of affliction, your teachers will be hidden

no more; with your own eyes
you will see them. Whether you turn to
the right or to the left, your ears will hear
a voice behind you, saying,
"This is the way; walk in it."

Thank you, Lord.
I trust you to show me the way.

ISAIAH 30:1-2,19-21

"Cursed is the one who trusts in man,
who depends on flesh for his strength
and whose heart turns away from the LORD.
He will be like a bush in the wastelands;
he will not see prosperity when it comes.
He will dwell in the parched places
of the desert, in a salt land where no one lives.
But blessed is the man who trusts in the LORD,
whose confidence is in him.
He will be like a tree planted by the water
that sends out its roots by the stream.
It does not fear when heat comes;
its leaves are always green.
It has no worries in a year of drought
and never fails to bear fruit."

JEREMIAH 17:5-8

49

THANK YOU FOR THE LOVE
OF MY HUSBAND

My husband is a good and decent man
who shelters and protects me,
giving generously from
his vast store of love.
I thank you for him, Lord!
He listens when I pour out
my heart to him, cradling me
in his arms in our bed as I speak of my
hopes, fears, regrets, dreams.
What would I do without this man?
He is your gift to me and to
our children, and though we've
had our hard times,
he has never wavered in
his commitment to me or to you.

Over the years I have watched him change,
acquiring greater patience and a deeper
capacity for intimacy.
I have watched you discipline
him, Lord, through difficult

bosses and obstinate secretaries,
through failure and heartache,
until he has given you everything.

You've done great work, Lord.
I like the result.

Father, continue to make us one.
Give us greater unity of mind, purpose,
and spirit.
Help us ever strive to be
compassionate, kind, humble,
gentle, and patient with each other.
And help me to forgive him
as quickly and completely
as he forgives me—
as you forgive us both.

Only then will *the peace of
Christ rule* in our hearts
and in our home.
What a gift marriage is, O Lord.
Thank you for this intimate
        and enduring union.

MATTHEW 19:5-6, COLOSSIANS 3:12-15

My lover spoke and said to me,
"Arise, my darling, my beautiful one,
and come with me."

SONG OF SONGS 2:10

I am my lover's and my lover is mine;
he browses among the lilies.

SONG OF SONGS 6:3

50

LORD, ARE YOU ANGRY WITH ME?

Lord, I can't help but think
you are sometimes angry with me—
over my hardness of heart, my unconfessed
sin, or my disobedience to your Word.
Then I feel so inadequate,
thinking I never measure up
to your expectations.
Like the psalmist, I ask, *Will
you be angry forever? How long
will your jealousy burn like fire?*

I need to cling to the truth of your Word,
which tells me that I have
peace with you through Jesus Christ.
That while I was powerless,
Christ died for me as a demonstration of
your great love.
*Since we have now been justified by
his blood, how much more shall we
be saved from God's wrath through him!*

I am not only saved from your anger but
reconciled to you, O Lord.
Even so, what do you see
when you look at me?

"Sing about a fruitful vineyard:
I, the LORD, watch over it;
I water it continually.
I guard it day and night
so that no one may harm it.
I am not angry.
If only there were briers
and thorns confronting me!
I would march against them in battle;
I would set them all on fire.
Or else let them come to me for refuge;
let them make peace with me,
yes, let them make peace with me."

Father, thank you that you are not
angry with me.
Thank you for your warmth, your grace,
and most of all,
your great love for me.

PSALM 79:5; ROMANS 5:1,6-11; ISAIAH 27:2-5

"I will not accuse forever, nor will I always be angry,
for then the spirit of man would grow faint before me—
the breath of man that I have created."

ISAIAH 57:16

51

LORD, MY MIND
IS TROUBLED TODAY

Lord, why does peace elude me?
Why this heavy weight upon my soul?

As Job said, *"My troubled*
thoughts prompt me to answer
because I am greatly disturbed."

My troubled mind keeps me awake nights.
I feel like the psalmist who said to you,
You kept my eyes from closing;
I was too troubled to speak.

Jesus was troubled and sorrowful
when he faced Gethsemane.
He said,
"My soul is overwhelmed with sorrow
to the point of death."
Even then, you gave him the
courage to go forward.
Lord, help me rest the full weight
of my cares upon you.

Thank you for Christ's words:
"Peace I leave with you;
my peace I give you.
I do not give to you
as the world gives.
Do not let your hearts
be troubled and do
not be afraid."

Lord, help me to keep my
mind fixed on you,
to experience your *perfect peace*
because I trust in you.

JOB 20:2, PSALM 77:4, MATTHEW 26:37-38,
JOHN 14:27, ISAIAH 26:3

God is just: He will pay back trouble to those who trouble
you and give relief to you who are troubled, and to us as
well. This will happen when the Lord Jesus is revealed
from heaven in blazing fire with his powerful angels.

2 THESSALONIANS 1:6-7

52

LORD, KEEP MY CHILDREN SAFE

The world has so much evil in it, Lord.
Daily I read or
hear accounts of little children
abducted,
abused,
killed—
harmed in some awful way.
My children need to have increasing freedom
as they grow—
I don't want them to retreat
from new experiences out of fear.
I trust them, Lord, but I
do not trust our culture.
Too many children are
growing up today
consumed by rage.
Neglected, abused, unloved,
they strike out.
Can I count on you to
protect my children, Lord?

"All your sons will be taught by the LORD,
and great will be your children's peace.
In righteousness you will be established:
Tyranny will be far from you;
you will have nothing to fear.
Terror will be far removed;
it will not come near you.
If anyone does attack you,
it will not be my doing;
whoever attacks you will
surrender to you.

"See, it is I who created the blacksmith
who fans the coals into flame
and forges a weapon fit for its work.
And it is I who have created
the destroyer to work havoc;
no weapon forged against
you will prevail,
and you will refute every tongue
that accuses you.
This is the heritage of
the servants of the LORD,
and this is their vindication from me."

Thank you, Father, for this assurance
of your constant care: you who hold
the universe in your hands
are certainly able to protect my children.

We will count on you,
our protector and defender.

ISAIAH 54:13-17

I will lie down and sleep in peace,
for you alone, O LORD, make me dwell
in safety.

PSALM 4:8

The name of the LORD is a strong tower;
the righteous run to it and are safe.

PROVERBS 18:10

53

HELP ME WITH MY IN-LAWS, LORD

I'm having difficulty
with my in-laws just now.
It's hard to juggle the
needs of my husband,
   children, parents,
   and extended family.
When I say no,
I have a hard time dealing with
our parents' responses.
I cringe when I hear the
disappointment in their voices.

I love these people, Lord, but sometimes
I just don't want to deal with them.
And when my mother-in-law
criticizes me, I don't always
   respond with love—letting
   her have her say but kindly
   and firmly telling her what
   my husband and I have
   decided to do.

Lord, I know you want us to love and
honor our parents.
Your Word tells me:
"Honor your father and your mother,
as the LORD your God has commanded you,
so that you may live long and that it may
go well with you in the land the LORD your God
is giving you."

But does honoring our parents mean always saying
    yes?
I think not.
We also honor our parents
by living honorable, compassionate, moral lives.

Teach me to set reasonable boundaries, Lord,
without feeling guilty.
To say *no* when necessary so that my *yes* will have
more meaning.
Help me to be a good daughter-in-law
without sacrificing my sanity
or my little family's peace.
Then I'll be better able to cherish and honor
these parents you have placed in my life.

DEUTERONOMY 5:16

If anyone does not provide for his relatives,
and especially for his immediate family,
he has denied the faith and is worse than
an unbeliever.

1 TIMOTHY 5:8

54

FATHER, MY FRIEND IS STRUGGLING WITH INFERTILITY

O Lord, my friend carries a heavy
burden just now.
She cried this morning because of years of
unanswered prayers,
dashed hopes,
insensitive questions from family and friends—
the strain of unfulfilled dreams.

She who longs to become a mother cannot.
I told her of your
compassion for women in the Bible who
struggled with infertility—
Sarah, Rebekah, Rachel, Hannah, Elizabeth.
They cried out to you, and
you responded to their distress.
Abraham and Sarah conceived
Isaac even when Sarah was too old
for anyone to believe she could possibly
bear a child.
Yet when Sarah questioned your
ability to give her a child,

you replied,
"Is anything too hard for the Lord?"

And when Isaac prayed to you
because his wife Rebekah was barren,
she, too, became pregnant—
the proud mother of sons.
Rachel, also, knew the pain
of the empty womb.
And Hannah, who despaired
of ever having children, was so distressed
she was unable to eat.
She prayed to you with great anguish and grief.
Years after you gave her Samuel, she sang:
"Those who were hungry
hunger no more.
She who was barren
has borne seven children."

Thank you, Lord, that you understand
how important children are to women—
that we gain a sense of significance
in becoming mothers.
Please hear my friend's prayer,
see her distress, and grant her her heart's desire.
May she soon experience the
joy of motherlove.

GENESIS 18:10-11,14; 25:21,24; 1 SAMUEL 1:7,16; 2:5

He settles the barren woman in her home
as a happy mother of children. Praise the LORD.

PSALM 113:9

55

FATHER, I FEEL GUILTY

Sometimes, O Lord, I am
overwhelmed by guilt for
things I have done in the past
to wrong you and others I love.
How it is that you
forgive me time and again?
I am like the psalmist
who said, *My guilt has
overwhelmed me like
a burden too heavy to bear.*

It seems I come to you repeatedly
for the same besetting sins.
When I stand before you, I am all too
conscious of the darkness in my heart.
Fear grabs me by the throat—
  what if you give me what I deserve
  for my sins against you and others?

Then your grace washes over me.
Tenderly, I hear your still, small voice:

"Forget the former things;
do not dwell on the past.
See, I am doing a new thing!
Now it springs up; do you
not perceive it?

"I, even I, am he who blots out
your transgressions, for my own sake,
and remembers your sins no more."

Thank you, Father, for reminding me
that even your prophet Isaiah felt guilty
when he came into your presence.
At that moment, he was terrifyingly aware of
his sinfulness, saying,
"Woe to me!... I am ruined! For I
am a man of unclean lips, and I
live among a people of unclean
lips, and my eyes have seen the
King, the LORD Almighty."
Then you sent a seraph
with a hot coal to touch
his lips, soothing him, telling him
that his sin had been atoned for,
his guilt taken away.

Thank you, Father, that
you minister to me,
just as you did to Isaiah.

"Though your sins are like scarlet,
they shall be as white as snow;
though they are red as crimson,
they shall be like wool."

You show me that the
Holy Spirit came into the world
to convict us of sin.
For the wages of sin is death,
but the gift of God is
eternal life in Christ Jesus our Lord.

Thank you, Lord, that my sins have been atoned for
and guilt no longer holds me as its thrall.

PSALM 38:4; ISAIAH 43:18-19,25; ISAIAH 6:5-7;
ISAIAH 1:18; JOHN 16:8; ROMANS 6:23

"For I will forgive their wickedness
and will remember their sins no more."

JEREMIAH 31:34

56

FORGIVE ME FOR GOSSIPING, LORD

Today I repeated something
to my friend that I should not have.
I told her about an argument I had
with a mutual friend.
Lord, when I have been wronged,
I want to rally others to
my defense.
I want to vindicate myself in my own eyes.
I always feel better when I hear
a friend say, "No, you
were right. She was wrong."

I know I was wrong
to malign my friend, Lord,
but sometimes I get sloppy about
the petty annoyances or minor
irritations that others inflict on me.
I find myself confiding these
things to my closest friend.
Help me to keep a tight rein on my
tongue and see this mutual

friend as you see her.
Your Word tells me that
a perverse man stirs up
dissension, and gossip separates
close friends.
Without wood a fire goes out;
without gossip a quarrel dies down.

I know you despise gossip, Lord.
Proverbs says you hate:
> *a lying tongue,*
> *a heart that devises wicked schemes,*
> *a false witness who pours out lies and*
> *a man who stirs up dissension among brothers.*

Lord, every word of yours is flawless.
Help me not to speak reckless words
that pierce the heart.
Instead, give me a tongue that
brings healing.
Forgive me for gossiping
about my friend today, Lord.
And the next time that natural tendency
rears its ugly head,
help me to think of life-giving
words instead.

PROVERBS 16:28, 26:20, 6:16-19, 30:5, 12:18

He who covers over an offense
promotes love,
but whoever repeats the matter
separates close friends.

PROVERBS 17:9

57

O FATHER, MY MARRIAGE SEEMS STALE AND FLAT THESE DAYS

As my husband and I go through our busy days
caring for children,
working,
paying bills,
living out the mundane, humdrum
aspects of our lives,
the marital fire slowly wanes.
What began as a blazing fire
now seems like glowing embers.

So little time for
      romance,
      heartfelt conversations,
      weekends away.
At the end of a long, exhausting day,
I just want to fall into bed.
Sex feels like one more task.

O Lord, rekindle our passion!

Solomon's lover
speaks of love that is

more delightful than wine.
She says
her beloved's name
is *like perfume poured out.*
How long has it been, O Lord,
since I felt that kind of passion
for my husband?

Help me meditate today
on the joys of marriage.
You created marriage and sexual intimacy,
not only to populate the earth,
but also as a hedge against loneliness.
Even when Adam was
naming all the creatures
of the earth, you saw that
there was no one suitable
for Adam.
You said:
"It is not good for the man to be alone.
I will make a helper suitable for him."
And so you created Eve.

Thus, the first marriage began.
And as a husband and wife
they experienced the first sexual union;
they became one flesh.

Thank you, Lord, for the
gift that is my marriage.

Help me to delight in my husband tonight
to enjoy the sexual bond we share,
to feast *among the lilies.*
To be bone of his bones
and flesh of his flesh.

SONG OF SONGS 1:2-3; GENESIS 2:20,18,24;
SONG OF SONGS 2:16; GENESIS 2:23

How much more pleasing is your love than wine,
and the fragrance of your perfume than any spice!

SONG OF SONGS 4:10

58

TODAY IS MY BIRTHDAY, LORD

Today I celebrate my birth, Lord.
Of course you know that—
you created me—
but as I awoke to sun streaming in
my bedroom and heard the
birds singing, my first
thoughts were of you.
Thank you, Father, that
I am alive today.
I rejoice that I am still on earth and that
I shall spend this day with
those who matter most:
      my husband, children,
      a few close women friends.

Even at those times when
I have suffered greatly,
you have always been with me,
sheltering me with your
vast store of love,
guiding me over sometimes difficult
terrain.

On those birthdays when I
was alone or lonely, wondering
if my parents rejoiced at my
birth, you became my nurturing
mother and father, telling
me that you loved me before
I was born—that my
birth was no accident.
For you created my inmost being;
you knit me together in my mother's womb.
I praise you because I am
fearfully and wonderfully made.
All of your works are
wonderful,
including me.

O Lord, it comforts me to know
that you will always know
where I am on my birthday—
I can never flee from your spirit.
If I were to go up to heaven
or descend to the depths of hell,
you would find me.
Your right hand will
hold me fast.
Close to your heart.
And before my mother
even gave birth, you had already
determined just how many
birthdays I would have on earth.

How wonderful this knowledge
is to me, O God.
Because I love you, I am
never alone.
You were with me at birth.
You will be with me in
death.
And I shall spend eternity
in your presence.

Thank you, Father, for all
my birthdays so far.
And today, as on other birthdays,
I will look for your birthday
greeting—in your Word and in
the love you send to me through
others.

"Can a mother forget the baby
at her breast and have no
compassion on the child she has borne?
Though she may forget,
I will not forget you!
See, I have engraved you
on the palms on my hands;
your walls are ever before me."

PSALM 139:13-14,8-10,16; ISAIAH 49:15-16

The LORD will fulfill his purpose for me;
your love, O LORD, endures forever—
do not abandon the works of your hands.

PSALM 138:8

59

JESUS, DO YOU HEAL TODAY?

Christ, you traveled to cities, villages,
      homes and synagogues,
teaching and preaching,
healing every manner of sickness
among those who thronged to you.
Sick, pained, terrified, they came—
the multitudes wanted only to touch you
and feel your healing power.

Because of your compassion, you healed
      Simon's mother-in-law,
      lepers,
      the paralytic,
      the centurion's servant.
You spoke, and sickness fled.
You cast out demons, and
the tormented were suddenly themselves.

Even death could not resist you.

When Jairus grieved the death
of his only daughter

and when the widow of Nain mourned
the passing of her only son and
when Mary and Martha were
devastated because of the demise
of their only brother, Lazarus,
you gave them back those they loved.
The grave was not strong
enough to hold on to those you
irresistibly called back to life.

Dear Jesus,
will you heal even me?
I, too, want to touch you,
to feel the healing power
flow out of you
and into my damaged body.
I know that you are able to
restore me to health,
to heal me from the inside out—
to mend my spirit as well as my body.

But will you?

Thank you, Jesus, that your Word
says you are *the same yesterday and
today and forever.*
The same compassionate
Savior and Healer.
Just as you healed
men and women long ago,

so you can heal me today.
In this present age.
You can send forth your Word
and heal me.
You can rescue me from the grave.
Heal me, O LORD, and I will be healed;
save me and I will be saved, for
you are the one I praise.

MATTHEW 9:35; LUKE 6:19; 4:38-39; 5:12-13,18-25; 7:2-10;

4:36,41; 8:49-55; 7:11-15; JOHN 11:4-44; HEBREWS 13:8;

PSALM 107:20; JEREMIAH 17:14

For great is your love toward me;
you have delivered me from the depths of the grave.

PSALM 86:13

60

LORD, I WANT TO PRAISE YOU

Today I feel exceedingly grateful.
For family.
For life.
For close, compassionate friends.
For meaningful work.
As I confront this day,
I am keenly aware of your goodness
to me and all who are earthbound.
The fact that we wake up in the morning
is a gift.
Because of the LORD's great love
we are not consumed,
for his compassions never fail.

O Father, I want to be like my friend
who struggled with cancer ten years ago
and who wakes up each day saying,
"Thank you, Lord, that I'm still here.
What do you want me to do today?"

Father, give me that same sense
of gratitude for life and breath—
that same sense of obedience
to your spirit.

Because your love is better than life,
my lips will glorify you.
I will praise you
as long as I live,
and in your name I will
lift up my hands.

May I come to know you in a deeper,
more intimate way as I try to
seek you with my whole heart.
Totality of commitment
pleases you.
Help me, Father,
to keep your laws and decrees
so that it may go well with me
and my children all the days of our lives
and I may someday enter your courts,
singing.

LAMENTATIONS 3:22; PSALM 63:3-4;

DEUTERONOMY 4:29,40; PSALM 100:4

I will praise you, O LORD, with all my heart;
I will tell of your wonders.
I will be glad and rejoice in you;
I will sing praise to your name, O Most High.

PSALM 9:1-2

SUBJECT INDEX

SUBJECT INDEX

ABOUT THE AUTHOR

Brenda Hunter, Ph.D., is a noted psychologist and an internationally published author. Her previous books include *The Power of Mother Love, Home by Choice, In the Company of Women, In the Company of Friends* (co-authored with her daughter Holly Larson), *What Every Mother Needs to Know about Babies,* and *A Wedding Is a Family Affair* (coauthored with her daughter Kristen Blair).

Hunter has appeared on television and radio programs nationwide, including *The Today Show, CBS This Morning, Focus on the Family,* and *Larry King Live,* and she has been profiled in the *Washington Post.*

Educated at Georgetown University, she has worked as a therapist with the Minirth, Meier and Byrd Counseling Center in Fairfax, Virginia. The mother of two grown daughters, Hunter lives in Virginia with her husband, Don.